ISBN 0.210.40570.8

77-111

PRINTED IN INDIA

AT ANANDA PRESS, LUCKNOW AND PUBLISHED BY
P.S. JAYASINGHE, ASIA PUBLISHING HOUSE, NEW YORK

PREFACE

DURING THE PAST two decades a large volume of literature regarding India's foreign relations has emerged. However, most of these studies are historical and descriptive in nature and rarely analytical or theoretical. This unevenness becomes rather critical when we look at the growing complexity in India's relations with her neighbours and the variety of her other international problems. Equally important is the fact that, in the years to come, India's international responsibilities and involvements are likely to grow rather than diminish. In order to meet these challenges, the Nation and its government must not only continuously reassess their foreign policy attitudes but also reevaluate the effectiveness of the decision and policy-making structure and system in terms of their capabilities and commitments. In other words, are the decision and policy-makers pursuing a defined and conscious goal and, if so, are they making the necessary resource commitment to develop the desired capability?

This study of Indian foreign policy pursues the line of inquiry, that it does, in order to present this complex material within certain theoretical framework. At times, the reader may detect some unfriendly comments in my presentation, but these are merely intellectual inquiries and not personal whims.

I am indebted to many persons and institutions who have helped in the preparation of this study. I would like specifically to acknowledge Dr. Ralph H. Smuckler, Dean of International Programs, Dr. William T. Ross, Director of Asian Studies Center, and Dr. C. L. Winder, Dean of the College of Social Science, all of Michigan State University, for their support and moral encouragement. Much of the research for this book was done in the serene surroundings of the Gandhi Peace Foundation at New Delhi during fall and winter of 1970-71, and I wish to thank its Secretary, Mr. Radha Krishna for permitting me to be a resident of the Foundation for an extended period. I am also appreciative of the generous help given by my secretary, Joyce Howard, enabling the completion of this study. Finally, I am deeply indebted to my wife

Barbara and my two sons Balkrishna and Balram who during the period of research have had many lonely months while I was away.

BALJIT SINGH

East Lansing, Michigan

CONTENTS

CHAPTER I

SOME THEORIES OF INTERNATIONAL POLITICS AND FOREIGN POLICY

A. THEORIES OF INTERNATIONAL POLITICS

MUCH HAS ALREADY been written about the importance of and need for theory in the field of international relations.[1] To a large extent, the concern voiced by students of international politics reflects their dissatisfaction with the nature of inquiries conducted when international relations first began to emerge as an independent field of study.

1. The Realist School

In 1946 Hans J. Morgenthau set off something of a revolution in international relations as well as political science. He suggested that all politics is the politics of interests, whether domestic or international, and power occupies a central position in the concept of national interest. Morgenthau, however, maintained that power relations are the *dominant*, but by no means the *only*, factor in international politics; they do not *control* all political actions.[2]

Morgenthau defined four purposes for the theory in international relations: (i) to serve as a tool for understanding and analysis, (ii) to provide justification for national decisions or actions, (iii) to serve as an intellectual conscience to remind the decision-makers of sound principles of foreign policy; and (iv) to prepare the ground for a new international order. Morgenthau maintained that international relations could not be reduced to a set of predictive propositions, because its contingent elements obviate the possibility of theoretical understanding.

Morgenthau advanced six propositions that constitute the basic beliefs of the realist school:[3] (a) Politics is governed by objective laws that stem from human nature (the laws by which man moves in the social world), and these laws are eternal. (b) Realism finds its main guide in the concept of interest defined in terms of power.

(*c*) Realism does not claim an absolute and permanent meaning for the concept of power; power must be constantly analyzed and weighed, and both the physical and psychological environments of an international situation must be taken into account to determine political action. (*d*) Realism is not indifferent to morality, but it is conscious that universal moral principles can not be realized; they can, at best, be approximated. (*e*) Realism does not recognize the moral aspirations of any particular nation as applicable to an international society; all nations are autonomous political actors, pursuing their interests defined according to their national power. (*f*) Realism is a distinctive intellectual approach and advocates the autonomy of politics from other spheres of human activity.

With regard to the motivations of men and nations, Morgenthau maintained the presence of two dominant elements: *selfishness* and *desire for power*. While selfishness is not without limits and therefore can be satisfied, the power drives of men and nations have no limits and cannot be satisfied or appeased by concessions. They can only be checked and controlled by the power drives of others; thus a system of balance of power is necessary to preserve order and peace in international relations.

Since the maintenance of international order and peace is the central goal of the realist theory of international relations, Morgenthau proposed two devices to obtain these ends: (*i*) balance of power and (*ii*) normative limitations of international law, international morality, and world public opinion. He found, however, that normative limitations are ineffective, and our only choice lies in a balance of power system.

Morgenthau classified historical attempts to attain peace into three categories: (*a*) limitation—disarmament, collective security, judicial settlement, etc.; (*b*) transformation—world state, etc.; and (*c*) accommodation—diplomacy. In his exmamination of the utility of these attempts, Morgenthau found that *limitation* has proved to be ineffective, and *transformation* was premature and unrealistic; only *accommodation*, i.e. diplomacy, held promise. Consequently, he emphasized diplomacy, and laid down nine guiding principles and rules for its conduct.[4] The importance of diplomacy, however, is that, by mitigating and minimizing conflicts, it contributes to the growth of a world community upon whose foundations a more secure and peaceful world, possibly through a world state, could be erected.

Morgenthau concluded by observing that knowledge, insight, and intuition were needed to carry on the work of peace and diplomacy. Scientific knowledge alone is not enough. "The insights and wisdom by which more-than-scientific man elevates his experience into the universal laws of human nature" were needed. All this called for *statesmen* in politics; *politicians* alone were not good enough.

Hans Morgenthau and the realist school of international relations have been criticized rather abundantly.[5] This criticism can be grouped into three general categories: (*i*) method, (*ii*) basic assumptions, and (*iii*) prescriptions.

His method is criticized on the ground that he starts with certain generalizations which he says are timeless and immune to change, and he supports his theses by quoting philosophers who supposedly possess insights. But other philosophers with equal insight can be quoted to challenge Morgenthau's generalizations. His method, consequently, is unscientific because his generalizations are not derived from critical experiments and cannot be verified.

Morgenthau's basic assumptions regarding power and self-interest are viewed as vague and imprecise. In a broad and general manner they explain *everything*, but in special and specific circumstances they may explain *nothing*. Because his assumptions are vague, his theory contains a single-factor (power) analytical framework, and therefore, like all single-factor theories, it has only limited value.

Finally, his prescription for the maintenance of international peace (diplomacy) is criticized on the ground of insufficient evidence. It is said that diplomacy as a tool for the preservation of international peace has seen a steady decline and there are still fewer signs to presume that it can stage a future comeback.*

2. *The Systemic School*

With the appearance of David Easton's *The Political System* in 1953, there began to emerge what has come to be known the *systemic*

---

*In the light of recent diplomatic successes relating to Vietnam (1973), Indo-Pakistan agreements (1972 and 1973) and other accords, these contentions do not appear to be well substantiated.

school in political science. Easton's stimulating study produced the inevitable *demonstration* effect upon the study of international relations as well, and reflected the discipline's desire to be *scientific*. During the following decade, while still in its formative stages, this school has made some notable contributions to our understanding of international political systems and promises the development of a scientific theory of international relations.[6]

The systemic school in international relations is compartmentalized into such branches as systems theory, decision-making theory, equilibrium theory, game theory, etc. Furthermore, the methods of inquiry vary and include survey research, content analysis, factor analysis, simulation, etc. As a result, unlike the *realist school*, the *systemic school* has yet to produce either a synthesis or a spokesman. However, in view of the short history of this school, its present state of development must be considered not only normal, but unavoidable, as these approaches are both comprehensive and complex and are designed to deal with an equally complex and fast changing international situation. Again, a great deal of attention has been focussed upon the development of theoretical frameworks, and correspondingly little has been done to gather the relevant data. This state of affairs has prompted censure from critics and has invited comments such as: "In the past, international relations was data rich and theory poor, while now it is theory rich and data poor." Even though the research during the past few years has been enormous, the *systemic school* does not appear to be on the verge of any major breakthrough regarding a general theory.[7]

In 1957, Morton Kaplan classified the international political system into six basic theoretical models:[8] (*i*) balance of power system; (*ii*) loose bipolar system; (*iii*) tight bipolar system; (*iv*) universal system; (*v*) hierarchical system; and (*vi*) unit veto system. He identified five variables within the models: (*a*) essential rules, (*b*) transformation rules, (*c*) actor classification, (*d*) capability, and (*e*) information.[9]

His models, however, where designed to explore the continuum of possibilities because only two out of the six models—the balance of power system and the loose bipolar system—could be identified in the real world. Despite this drawback, Kaplan's study was considered a major contribution and supposedly enriched the possibilities of a systematic analysis of world politics.

In a recent article,[10] Morton Kaplan has advanced *four* additional models of international system: (*i*) very loose bipolar system; (*ii*) the detente system; (*iii*) the unstable bloc system; and (*iv*) incomplete nuclear diffusion system. Even though these may be considered variations of his earlier models, a further precision is evident, and to this extent these additional models are a worthwhile effort. However, these international systems do not help in the analysis of the environment prevalent in the real world.[11]

3. *A Critique of International Political Systems*

The foregoing discussion has dealt primarily with the development of theory in international relations, i.e. the *realist* and the *systemic* theories. The drawbacks of the *realist* theory as presented by Hans Morgenthau have already been pointed out. Now I shall attempt to evaluate the *systemic* model as developed by Morton Kaplan in terms of its methods and its promise for the development of a general theory of International relations.

In order to understand better and analyze the logic of science, i.e. methodology, we must first understand what an empirical science is. Clarifying the meaning of "science" is tantamount to determining the criteria for the distinction between warranted and unwarranted assertions, in other words, to explicating the principles of scientific control. What are these scientific controls ? Briefly, they are the following:

1. The ideal of unity and simplicity, i.e. laws arranged in a hierarchy. The number of independent variables is small and their mathematical relations are simple.
2. The ideal of unrestricted universality, i.e. the highest laws of the system must be temporally and numerically unrestricted. Certain more specific laws are subject to variations.
3. The ideal of precision, i.e. restriction of the frames of possibility. The laws should be established in metrical relations among the facts to which they refer. All genuine laws, therefore, have a mathematical form. Science, accordingly, is given the task of replacing qualitative thought with quantitative data.
4. The ideal of the pervasiveness of law, i.e. no class of facts not falling under the law, and no class of indeterminable factors.

Ideally, a scientific theory of international relations must conform to these standards. These alone do full justice to the austere demands of scientific inquiry: the formulation of precise, simple laws that permit reliable predictions. I am, however, aware that the subject-matter of international relations is more complicated than that of a natural science; we have to operate with data that are not controllable and hence cannot exhibit as strict and rigid a set of laws as those in the natural sciences. Furthermore, the amorphous and constantly changing field of international relations does not even possess the clarity of terminology required of strict scientific inquiry. The ambiguity of such terms as freedom, self-determination, offensive and defensive weapons, etc. has led to rather unceasing controversies about their "true" meaning. Often the same words have altogether different connotations to various sets of people living under different political institutions.

Being conscious and appreciative of the difficult tasks that lie in the path of a scientific or a general theory of international relations, I must, nevertheless, raise some questions regarding Morton Kaplan's models of the international systems. To begin with, I agree with a general comment by Charles Boasson regarding Morton Kaplan's *System and Process in International Politics.* He said: "I must admit that I have not been able to determine what system and what process we can, on Mr. Kaplan's advice, select, or what 'sub-systems' we can extract from the international scene.... [T] his vagueness is not merely or mainly because of his overcomplicated language, but because of the intrinsic vagueness... of the recognizable factors in international decision-making and situations, and the further vaguenss of their mutual inter-relatedness, so that rigidly precise theory becomes inappropriate.... [H] is full inventory of alternative is... of doubtful use, not only for the predictive purposes which their author mentions as a future hope, but even for the purpose of gaining a more general insight and understanding."[12]

Even though this criticism was advanced before Kaplan expanded his list of international systems from six to ten,[13] it still remains a valid objection. Of the initial six, *only two* models—the balance of power system and the loose bipolar system—can be identified in the real world. The recent four additional models were developed mainly by Professor Kaplan's students in the process of working on their doctoral dissertations and are, by and

'arge, cataloguing endeavours; they make no theoretical advance-
ment. For instance, Morton Kaplan now has four of his systems,
namely, loose bipolar system, very loose bipolar system, unstable
bloc system, and incomplete nuclear diffusion system, distinguish-
ing themselves more by their operative styles than by their
theory or methodology. Similar objections can be justifiably raised against his two other systems, balance of power system and the
detente system.

My main objection, however, arises from the consideration that
none of Professor Kaplan's existing ten international systems are
applicable to the contemporary world scene in any meaningful
manner. In all modesty, I am compelled to say that in my review
of the various theories of international relations, I have, on balance, found Morgenthau's theoretical framework more meaningful and generally applicable and other model as rather distracting
and inappropriate. As we shall later on see, the foreign policy
of India can be analyzed better in terms of interests and power
than through idealistic or systemic theories.

B. A NOTE ON THEORIES OF FOREIGN POLICY

Unlike the theories of international politics, the theorization in
the field of foreign policy is somewhat recent.[14] From an occasional chapter in the textbooks on international relations or a
mere recommendation, it has now emerged as separate field of
study, though understandably it is still an aspect of the larger
subjects of national and international politics. For convenience,
the various theories on the subject can be grouped into two categories: (i) General Theories, and (ii) Middle-Range or Partial
Theories. In the first category are included theories such as
(a) Analytical; (b) Structural-Functional; and (c) Decision-making.
The middle-range theories can more appropriately be described as
analytical tools and include studies on: (i) Public opinion and related
fields of mass communication; (ii) Official actors such as specific
governmental agencies, the legislative and executive branches of
government; and (iii) Unofficial individuals or groups, often called pressure groups, acting in the process.

One can readily recognize that most thories of foreign policy
had their origins in other fields, mainly, economics, psychology,
and other behavioural sciences. I make this point to emphasize

that these non-indigenous approaches need to be adopted with considerable care. Any wholesale application can produce misleading consequences and is disservice to the subject under examination.

Any detailed discussion of the various theories of foreign policy is outside the scope of this study. I shall only briefly discuss the analytical approach to foreign policy, because I have attempted to examine the foreign policy of India within this framework. My analysis, however, considerably departs from the formal analytical theory and bears the heavy 'realist' imprint a la Morgenthau.

The analytical approach concentrates upon the elements and objectives of foreign policy and considers them to be the results of a variety of factors, attitudes, and circumstances. A nation's foreign policy reflects some unalterable foundations embodied in national character and aspirations. Some may consider this view a rather traditional way of looking at things, but the contemporary analytical approach goes beyond the traditional "national interest" approach and emphasizes the inherent impossibility of predicting foreign policy courses. The theory proposes that foreign policy is a "social process" and its direction is considerably shaped by an interplay of economic, military, ideological, and other factors both within and among nations.

The essential elements of this approach are contained in the hypothesis that foreign policy is a system of activities evolved by nations for influencing and changing the behaviour of other states and for adjusting their own activities to the international environment. Foreign policy is not the product of men sitting in offices making rational choices but rather a complex social process in which (i) policy-makers, (ii) principles of foreign policy, (iii) policy aims, interests and objectives, (iv) power-inputs and outputs, and (v) the context of foreign policy, all play an interacting and related role.

Power-inputs and outputs, interests, and objectives are the main variables in this approach. Power is considered the product of cooperation between the policy-makers and their community. The role of policy-maker is to process power-inputs into effective power-outputs. The demands made by the community are called "interests," and when they are incorporated into foreign policy they become "objectives." This sequence is deemed to be a desirable behaviour of states. All these actions, of course, are guided by certain "principles." Any changes in these elements or in the relationship among them will produce changes in the whole sphere of foreign policy. Such a change will also produce changes in other parts of the international system. Therefore, foreign policy-making is the constant adaptation and adjustment to changing relationships among the component variables. Consequently, it should be viewed as a "process" rather than something mechanical or static.

NOTES

1 For further comments on this see: Charles A. McClelland, *Theory and the International System* (New York: Macmillan Company, 1966), pp. 1-30; Horace V. Harrison, ed., *The Role of Theory in International Relations* (Princeton, N.J. : D. Van Nostrand Company, Inc., 1964); Stanley Hoffman, ed., *Contemporary Theory in International Relations* (Englewood Cliffs, N.J. : Prentice-Hall, Inc., 1960); and William T.R. Fox, ed., *Theoretical Aspects of International Relations* (Notre Dame : University of Notre Dame Press, 1959).

2 For the central concepts of Morgenthau's theory of international relations, see: *Scientific Man Versus Power Politics* (Chicago: University of Chicago Press, 1946); and *In Defence of National Interest* (New York: Alfred Knopf, 1951). For an application of the theory, see: *Politics Among Nations* (New York: Alfred Knopf, 3rd edition, 1960).

3 These six propositions are interspersed in most of Morgenthau's writings on the subject. The most succinct presentation, however, is available in his *Scientific Man Versus Power Politics*. For a valuable and concise presentation of Morgenthau's theory of international relations, see: Ghazi A. R. Algosaibi, "The Theory of International Relations: Hans J. Morgenthau and His Critics," *Background* 8: 4 (Feb., 1965), pp. 221-256.

4 For a detailed discussion of these rules, see his *Politics Among Nations* (3rd edition), pp. 560-568.

5 For further criticisms, see: Benno Wasserman, "The Scientific Pretentions of Professor Morgenthau's Theory of Power Politics," *Australian Outlook*, 13 (March, 1959), pp. 55-70; Kenneth Waltz, in review of *Dilemmas of Politics*, *American Political Science Review*, 53: 2 (June, 1959), p. 531; Richard Snyder, "International Relations Theory—Continued," *World Politics*, 13: 2 (January, 1961), pp. 300-312; Stanley Hoffmann, "International Relations: The Long Road to Theory," in James N. Rosenau, ed., *International Politics and Foreign Policy* (Glencoe, Illinois: Free Press, 1961), pp. 421-537; and Robert Tucker, "Professor Morgenthau's Theory of Political 'Realism'," *APSR*, 46: 1 (March, 1952), pp. 214-224.

6 Among the more thought-provoking studies in the systemic school, the following deserve mention: Morton A. Kaplan, *System and Process in International Politics* (New York: John Wiley and Sons, 1957); and Richard Rosecrance,

Action and Reaction in World Politics: International Systems in Perspective (Boston: Little, Brown & Company, 1963), for the systems approach. Richard Snyder, H.W. Bruck, and Burt Sapin, *Foreign Policy Decision-Making: An Approach to the Study of International Politics* (New York: Free Press, 1962); and Richard Snyder and James A. Robinson, *National and International Decision-Making* (New York: The Institute for International Order, 1961), for the decision-making approach. Also see: George Liska, *International Equilibrium: A Theoretical Essay on the Politics and Organization of Security* (Cambridge, Mass. : Harvard University Press, 1957); and Thomas C. Schelling, *The Strategy of Conflict* (New York: Oxford University Press [Galaxy Paperback], 1963), for the equilibrium and game theory approaches, respectively.

[7] The bibliography of writings on the subject is considerable. However, as an example of the recent approaches see: Steven J. Brams, "Transaction Flows in the International System," *The American Political Science Review*, LX : 4 (December, 1966), pp. 880-898. The author applies a variety of complex mathematical formulae and informs the reader that trade transaction flows in the international system are determined by (1) geographical proximity, and (2) ex-colonial ties.

[8] Morton A. Kaplan, *System and Process in International Politics* (New York: John Wiley & Sons, 1957), Chapter 2.

[9] *Ibid*, p. 9.

[10] Morton A. Kaplan, "Some Problems of International Systems Research," in *International Political communities—An Anthology* (Garden City, N. Y. : Double day & Company, Inc., 1966) (Anchor), pp. 469-501.

[11] For a critique of the systemic approach see Stanley H. Hoffmann, "International Relations: The Long Road to Theory," in James N. Rosenan, ed., *International Politics and Foreign Policy: A Reader in Research and Theory* (New York: Free Press, 1961), pp. 421-437; and Jay S. Goodman, "The Concept of System in International Relations Theory," *Background;* 8: 4 (February, 1965), pp. 257-268.

[12] Charles Boasson, *Approaches to the Study of International Relations* (Assen, The Netherlands : Van Gorcum, (1963), p. 80.

[13] *International Political Communities.*

[14] For a discussion of various theories see: Bernard C. Cohen, *The Influence of Non-governmental Groups on Foreign Policy-Making* (Boston: World Peace Foundation, 1959); and *The Press and Foreign Policy* (Princeton, N.J. : Princeton University Press, 1963); Joseph Frankel, *The Making of Foreign Policy* (New York: Oxford University Press, 1963); Feliks Gross, *Foreign Policy Analysis* (New York: Philosophical Library, 1954); George Liska, *International Equilibrium* (Cambridge, Mass. : Harvard University Press, 1957); Kurt London, *The Making of Foreign Policy: East and West* (New York: J.B. Lippencott Co., 1965); George A. Modelski, *Theory of Foreign Policy* (New York: Frederick A. Praeger, 1961); and Harold and Margaret Sprout, *Man-Milieu-Relationship Hypotheses in the Context of International Politics* (Princeton, N.J. : Center for International Studies, Princeton University, 1956).

CHAPTER II

SOME BASIC FACTORS

THE BASIC FACTORS that determine India's foreign relations can be grouped into *geographic, economic, social,* and *ideological* and *political* categories. They do not always operate in any calculable manner. Individual perceptions and reactions by elites to developments in other parts of the world often enter into the decisions of the national government. But for the sake of a general understanding we can assume that most decisions are the product of a rational and pragmatic weighing of the factors given above.

A. GEOGRAPHICAL FACTORS

Despite the towering Himalayas flanking the nation's northern and north-eastern frontiers, India, in this age of jet travel and nuclear tipped missiles, is an exposed country. Its extensive coastline, stretching over 3,000 miles, includes three main bodies of water—the Arabian Sea, the Bay of Bengal, and the Indian Ocean. India's strategic location has placed it within easy reach of many sensitive areas in the world including China, the Southeast Asian nations, West Asia, and East Africa. In practical terms these nations and regions spell ambition and power (China), raw materials and other mineral wealth (South East Asia and East Africa), and oil and strategic location (West Asia). Furthermore, India cannot afford to be just an observer of the future developments in these regions. Not only will the development in these areas affect her own course politically, but more importantly, a strong and industrialized India should, and in fact may soon need to, cooperate with many of her neighbours for raw materials to develop her industrial capacities.

Beyond the immediate regions, India is also on the trade route to Japan and the nations of the Western world. The Suez Canal ties her with Mediterranean nations and the European continent. Mr. Nehru once remarked:

We are in a strategic part of Asia, set in the centre of the
Indian Ocean, with intimate past and present connections
with Western Asia, Southeast Asia, and Far Eastern Asia.
Even if we could we would not want to ignore this fact. . . .[1]

India's geographical location, therefore, bears heavily upon her
security. These different trade routes and adjoining borders must
remain friendly and accessible at all times and must seek to move
toward greater economic, social, cultural, and political cooperation in the future. For that is what the current situation more
or less dictates.

B. ECONOMIC FACTORS

Despite some significant gains in the fields of industry, agriculture,
and commerce, India continues to remain a backward nation or,
in the parlance of current phraseology, a "developing country."
Perhaps the most critical of these economic factors are India's
overwhelming population and its heavy dependence on agriculture. By way of comparison, while India is roughly two-fifths of
the size of the United States, it has more than two and one half
time the population. More significantly, while less than six per
cent of the population of the United States is engaged in agriculture and produces more than abundant quantities of food, some
eighty per cent of India's population is engaged in feeding the
nation. Even then, success in the venture is heavily dependent
upon the whims of nature.

The ever-growing population of India (from 360 million in 1947
to 540 million in 1970) continues to nullify whatever economic
progress the country registers in other sectors such as industry and
commerce. Ironically, much of the increase in population is attri-
butable to better health care, lower infant mortality, and hence
a longer life span.

The problem of feeding such a sizable population, while trying
to form and maintain an organized society and bring social justice
and economic and cultural progress, can present enormous
strains and stresses on any government. In this context, one must
appreciate the fortitude and determination which Indian leaders
from Mr. Nehru to Mrs. Gandhi have continued to display.

Generally speaking, India's natural resources are diversified

SOME BASIC FACTORS   13

and relatively abundant. A steady pace of peaceful development coupled with population control can make the country self-sufficient in 'most of her economic needs in approximately fifteen to twenty years. While the success of population control is largely up to the people and government of India, the maintenance of peace in the international community depends upon a variety of external factors. The economic necessities, consequently, remain a major factor determining the nation's outlook in her international relations. Ever since the days of Mr. Nehru, India has been searching for security and stability, but needless to say, these attempts toward peace have not been always successful.

That economic factors do heavily influence the foreign policy of India remains to be an undisputed phenomenon however often it is denied at various levels of government. In operational terms, India's five-year plans for economic development require the assistance of many developed nations with differing ideologies and institutions. It was only pragmatic that India chose to remain politically non-aligned to serve her best interests. As to the advantages of political or military alliances to receive economic assistance, Mr. Nehru once remarked:

Even in accepting economic help, or in getting political help, it is not a wise policy to put all your eggs in one basket. Nor shall one get help at the cost of one's self-respect. Then you are not respected by any party ; you may get some petty benefits, but ultimately even these may be denied you.[2]

The observations of Nehru, even today, remain sound and practical. India's economic needs within the context of international politics underscore the basic correctness of this policy.

C. SOCIAL FACTORS

In this category we can include a host of social factors centering on caste, ethnicity, regionalism, language, and religion. But I would like to emphasize only two factors, regionalism and religion, since they have a direct bearing upon the nation's foreign policy inasmuch as they generate considerable strain upon national unity.

Despite the current slogan "unity in diversity," India's democracy is still young, and her regional and religious traditions and cultures are old and diverse. Political, economic and administrative unity have been well established for some time, but only as a superstructre. The infrastructure upon which national unity can be firmly established is still very fragile. Some important components of this infrastructure are a sense of common national goals, emotional integration, and religious tolerance and brotherhood.

For a variety of geographic, cultural, and communication reasons, people in different regions of India look at the nation in peculiar ways. People in the north, especially in Punjab, Jammu and Kashmir indentify with those from the central Asian culture. Their styles of dress, food habits and artistic and cultural heritage reinforce their beliefs. In some ways they have more in common with adjoining foreign nations than with their own countrymen from Bengal and Tamil Nadu. This compliment is more or less returned by the people of Bengal and Tamil Nadu in their attitude toward the people of the northern states. Similarly, their prolonged isolation from the main centres of activity in the country has only rarely given the people of hill regions, both in the Ladakh and the Northeast, a sense of belonging to India. Yet, these are some of the most sensitive regions where India continues to be in conflict with foreign powers.

The threat of regionalism often takes the form of linguistic and even religious differences. As far as the linguistic factor is concerned, the country through the reorganization of states on linguistic lines has made necessary amendments and what was once considered the most serious danger[3] has been elevated to a higher level of conflict, the competing demands for scarce economic resources. However, the religious diversity and antagonism remain, and it is here that the real dangers to national unity lie.

Among all the religious diversity in India, the differences among the Hindus and the Muslims remain the most pronounced. With the creation of Pakistan as a homeland for Muslims, this schism has taken on a political dimension as well. A strong national unity is impossible as long as the two major religious communities of India stay apart, and tolerance alone is not enough. Active participation in positive programmes is required, but it will remain an elusive commodity unless Hindus and Muslims educate themselves in the art of separating religion (a personal phenomenon) from politics (a community affair). Moreover, Pakistan's occasional intrusion into Hindu-Muslim differences in India as the spokesman of the Muslims in the subcontinent has only aggravated an already bad situation.

It is imperative that Indian politics embrace a genuinely secular style. The survival of the Republic may someday hang in balance because it was not secular enough or democratic enough or both.

D. IDEOLOGICAL AND POLITICAL FACTORS

While the three preceding categories of factors are, by and large, products of geography, economy and history, the ideological and political determinants of Indian foreign policy, more than anything else, are the products of the nation's own choosing. This is not to say that no social or historical compulsions are ascertainable, but merely to point out that these decisions were conscious and were made from a number of available alternatives.

The basic ideological themes in India's foreign policy appear to be : (*i*) national self-determination, (*ii*) anti-colonialism, (*iii*) non-interference in other nation's affairs, (*iv*) promotion of international peace, and (*v*) peaceful cooperation among nations for mutual benefit. The political framework within which India has sought to pursue these aims is that of ''non-alignment.''[4]

Ever since India's independence, the foreign policy of India has been the handiwork of one man—Jawaharlal Nehru. Even after his death, the essential elements of his world view remain the guiding principles of India's foreign policy. In many ways, Nehru was more than the Prime Minister and Foreign Minister, for he shaped the nation's thinking on world affairs and made India conscious of the momentous developments taking place in the world community. The outside world, in turn, considered Nehru more than the leader of India and listened to him as the voice of the emerging new nations of the world. In a period of transitional international politics, when the pattern of relations between the old and the new nations of the world was being rearranged, Nehru, as the spokesman not only of India but of the Afro-Asian nations, had considerable stature in the world. He came to be identified as an enlightened statesman belonging to the entire international community and hence was considered to be a bridge between the East and the West, between the old and the new.

In his first statement outlining India's foreign policy, Nehru remarked:

> We propose, as far as possible, to keep away from the power politics of groups, aligned agninst one another, which have led in the past to world wars and which may again lead to disasters on an even vaster scale. We believe that peace and freedom are indivisible and the denial of freedom anywhere must endanger freedom elsewhere and lead to conflict and war. We are particularly interested in the emancipation of colonial and dependent countries and peoples, and in the recognition in theory and practice of equal opportunity for all races.... [5]

Nehru also extended the hand of friendship and cooperation to all the nations of the world, particularly to the countries of British Commonwealth, the United States of America, and the Soviet Union.

His remakrs regarding countries of Asia, however, were much more warm and personal. He recalled that :

> We are of Asia and the peoples of Asia are nearer and closer to us than others. India is so situated that she is the pivot of Western, Southern, and South-East Asia. In the past her culture flowed to all these countries and they came to her in many ways. Those contacts are being renewed and the future is bound to see a closer union between India and South-East Asia on the one side, and Afghanistan, Iran, and the Arab world on the other. To the furtherance of that close association of free countries we must devote ourselves.... [6]

And expressing his good wishes toward China, then ravaged by the civil war, Nehru said :

> China, that mighty country with a mighty past, our neighbour, has been our friend through the ages and that friendship will endure and grow. We earnestly hope that her present troubles will end soon and an united democratic China will emerge, playing a great part in the furtherance of world peace and progress. [7]

From this statement evolved the concrete foreign policy assumed by the Nehru government for many subsequent years.

These policies, of course, were often reassessed and were articulated in different styles by Nehru, Krishna Menon and others, but the basic framework altered little. Non-alignment and peaceful coexistence came to be "the two most important goals of Indian foreign policy." As is well known, these policies had many critics, both at home and abroad. Nehru staunchly defended his policies as just and proper for India. In an address at Columbia University, New York, on October 17, 1949, Nehru said :

> I am asked frequently why India does not align herself with a particular nation or a group of nations and told that because we have refrained from doing so we are sitting on the fence. The question and the comment are easily understood, because in times of crises it is not unnatural for those who are involved in it deeply to regard calm objectivity in others as irrational, short-sighted, negative, unreal, or even unmanly. But I should like to make it clear that the policy India has sought to pursue is not a negative and neutral policy. It is a positive and a vital policy that flows from our struggle for freedom and from the teaching of Mahatma Gandhi....When man's liberty or peace is in danger we cannot and shall not be neutral; neutrality then would be a betrayal of what we have fought for and stand for.[3]

It can be argued that the ideological and political framework of Indian foreign policy was Nehru's conscious and deliberate creation, that the guiding principles in these decisions were pragmatic and expedient, and that, in the absence of an organized opinion on world affairs, Nehru was equally free to choose other courses of action for the nation's foreign policy. On closer examination, however, this view is not convincing. It is true that Nehru, as the undisputed supreme leader of the Indian people, could have moulded his people's thinking. But it is also true that the essential character of the Indian people, steeped in their religious, cultural and historical traditions, is not aggressive and warlike. Any policy that smacked of power politics was unlikely to arouse any enthusiasm or support. Nehru might have been forced to stand alone [away from the temper of his people], and the necessary human element for the success for such a policy would have been hard to obtain. Being the leader of the masses that he was, Nehru referred to his country's tradition of peaceful coexistence in a speech at Calcutta on November 30, 1955, in the following manner:

> It has been our way of life and is as old as our thought and culture. About 2,200 years ago, a great son of India, Ashoka, proclaimed it and inscribed it on rock and stone, which exist today and give us his message. Ashoka told us that we should respect the faith of others and that a person who extols his own faith and decries another faith injures his own faith. This is the lesson of tolerance and peaceful coexistence and cooperation which India has believed in through the ages. In the old days, we talked of religion and philosophy; now we talk more of the economic and social system. But the approach is the same now as before. That is the reason why we try to be friendly with all countries whether we agree with them or not. That is the reason why we refrain from criticizing other countries even when we disagree with their policies, unless circumstances compel us to explain our viewpoint.[9]

The pursuit of *panchsheela* (the five principles of Peace incorporating the ideological factors) within the political framework of non-alignment continues to remain ingrained in Indian foreign policy. Despite some debate and occasional criticism, Nehru's successors have defended it as the most sensible and correct policy for India. The test of a policy, however, lies in its ability to achieve desired results. India's degree of success will be examined in the following chapters when we discuss some concrete aspects of her national interests.

NOTES

[1]   Quoted in Karunakar Gupta, *Indian Foreign Policy: In Defence of National Interest* (Calcutta : The World Press (P) Ltd. 1956), p. 1.

[2]   Speech in the Parliament on March 8, 1948. Reproduced in S. L. Poplai, ed. *India: 1947-1950*, vol. II (London : Oxford University Press), 1959, p. 27.

[3]   For further discussion see, Selig S. Harrison, *India: The Most Dangerous Decades* (Princeton, N. J. : Princeton University Press, 1961).

4 For a detailed discussion see, J. C. Kundra, *Indian Foreign Policy 1947-1954.* (Groningen : J. D. Walters, 1955) ; Michael Brecher, *Nehru: A Political Biography* (New York : Oxford University Press, 1956); Karunaker Gupta, *Indian Foreign Policy.* Tibor Mende, *Nehru: Conversations on India and World Affairs* (New York : G. Braziller, 1956); Jawaharlal Nehru, *India's Foreign Policy: Selected Specches—September 1946-April 1961* (Delhi : Publications Division, Government of India, 1961); and S. R. Patel, *Foreign Policy of India: An Inquiry and crititism* (Bombay, M. M. Tripathy. 1960).

5 Broadcast from New Delhi, November 7, 1946. Quoted in *Jawaharlal Nehru on World Affairs—1946-64* (New Delhi : Indian Council of World Affairs, 1964), p. 76.

6 *Ibid.*

7 *Ibid.*

8 *Ibid.*, p. 78.

9 *Ibid.*

CHAPTER III

INDIA AND THE SUPER POWERS

INDIA'S FOREIGN POLICY, as expressed by its framers, appears to be drawn into three concentric circles. The outermost of these circles deals with the world's super powers, i. e. the United States and the Soviet Union. The middle circle encompasses the emergent "third world" nations of Asia, Africa, and Latin America. The innermost circle applies to India's immediate neighbours—Pakistan, China, Nepal, etc. One cannot always draw very neat lines of distinction between these three areas of policy because in the world of international politics no such separate packages exist in isolation. All international developments, even some internal developments, produce widespread reactions. Thus Indo-Pakistani relations affect Indo-Soviet and Indo-U. S. relations. Similarly, Sino-Soviet relations affect Indo-U. S.-Pakistani relations, and so on. Nevertheless, considering Indian foreign policy in this framework does have the merit of enabling us to examine the various concerns of the nation according to their differing importance and emphasis. After all, a rightist *coup d'etat* in Chile, however deplorable, cannot be as important to India as the emergence of, for example, a pro-Peking government in Nepal. So, mindful of the complexity of international politics, let us look first at the outermost circle, embracing India and the super powers.

A. NON-ALIGNMENT

In discussing India's relations with the super powers I am reminded of the story told by K. P. S. Menon, India's Ambassador to the Soviet Union in the 1950's. At a banquet held in the Kremlin in June, 1955, in honour of Nehru, Nicolai Bulganin, then Soviet Prime Minister, proposed a toast to Indo-Sovit friendship and said : "If we Russians, are friends, we are friends unto death; and if we are enemies, we are enemies unto death." In reply, Nehru expressed his appreciation of the Soviet friendship for India but added : "We, Mr. Prime Minister, have no enemies."[1]

Those words today sound not only ironic but unreal. But Nehru sincerely believed in them and had based his foreign policy on the assumption that India had no enemies. In fact, India could be a friend to all nations, irrespective of the social, economic, ideological, or political differences between them.

Until 1947, India's foreign relations were handled exclusively by the British Government, initially from Whitehall and later, during the last years of their rule, through the India Office in London. So when India became independent, the Nehru government had no inhibitions or obstacles to starting afresh and devising a foreign policy without any inherited animosities or prejudices. India's emergence as an independent nation also coincided with the rise of the United States and the Soviet Union as the two super powers, each with an almost fanatic righteousness towards their ideology, way of life, and foreign policies. Even at that early date it was apparent that these two opposing views would one day collide, as indeed they did, in Berlin, then in Korea, Greece, and other places around the globe. Each power soon set up military blocs resulting in NATO, CENTO, SEATO, Anzus, and Warsaw Pact.

This emerging patterns of relations between the super powers was a disquieting phenomenon and left India only limited posssibilities for action.[2] Nehru could have chosen either to join one bloc or the other or to stay neutral. He chose non-alignment because it provided not only flexibility of action but also the opportunity to play a positive role in the cause of peace. India could be of service in times of need as a bridge to East-West understanding. In this limited context, Nehru's assessment of India's role as a non-aligned nation proved to be correct. India played an active role in bringing the two adversaries to some sort of compromises in Korea, Indo-China, and in the Congo crises. India's interpretations of the policies and sentiments of the two super powers to each other were another positive contribution toward a rapprochment between the United States and the Soviet Union. In a critical period of history India's policy of non-alignment served the cause of peace. These were laudable achievements and must be recognized as such.

Even though Nehru did not consider non-alignment a means for obtaining aid from all sides, the economic benefits to the country have been many. Both American and Soviet assistance has been substantial as has aid from other countries from both the blocs. All this is well and good but the policy of non-alignment can be reviewed in a different manner as well. To begin with, it can be argued that non-alignment, in itself, is not a policy. At best, it is a frame of reference within which certain foreign policy attitudes evolve. The late Rammanohar Lohia, the maverick socialist leader, in a speech in *Lok Sabha* in August 1963, commenting upon the government's foreign relations, remarked : "One minister of this government clings to the United States, another to Russia, and the Magician [Nehru] tries to hold the balance by his charm. They call this non-alignment."

A foreign policy is neither a singular nor an abstract phenomenon. It is a concrete set of objectives pursued through well determined and clearly defined channels. In other words, the goals of a nation must be arranged in some order of priority, and their pursuit must be backed through all necessary resource commitment. And if a nation's policy objectives and resources do not correlate acceptably, then the nation needs either to curtail its policy objectives or to increase its resource commitment. Nehru himself indicated an awareness of this proposition when he said :

Any part we want to play in world affairs depends entirely on the internal strength, unity, and conditions in our country. Our views might create some impression on others for this moment but they will attach importance to our voice only in proportion to the strength they know we have. Therefore, both from the point of view of our primary needs and from the point of view of any desire we might have to play a part in world affairs, we have to pay the first attention to our own country's affairs.[3]

If Nehru meant what he said, one is then compelled to ask : 'why attempt to organize India's international relations according to a Grand Design, where the farthest concentric circle in the nation's foreign policy objectives assumed the most importance and the issues and problems closest to the country's interests were relegated to a lower status ? As indicated earlier, it is true that some correlation does exist between both national and international politics, and international politics at different levels, but it is plainly absurd to assume that the solution to a nation's internal problems lies somewhere in the international arena. The Japanese example is an eloquent refutation of this assumption.

This is not a cirticism of the *idea* of non-alignment, as the policy was perhaps best suited to India's needs in the earlier days of her independence. What I am critical of is the whole set of unrealistic priorities that engaged the attention of national leaders, particularly Nehru. It is self-satisfying to keep talking of the laudatory role played by India in international crises during the 1950s. But what does it mean in terms of India's preparedness to meet her economic and national security needs? Nehru's remarks at the Kremlin reception, quoted earlier, cannot be viewed as anything more than gracious diplomacy. A man of Nehru's knowledge and understanding of history could not have had any such illusions. And were he under such illusions, they should have been thoroughly shattered during the 1962 India-China border war. (Parenthetically, Nehru should have anticipated this development, because at least as early as 1958, he had certain classified facts indicating that China's designs against Indian territory were hostile). But instead of some fresh, bold thinking on matters of national policies, India's leaders, after the initial shock of India-China conflict was over, struggled hard to return to their own unreal world.

The old, tired solgans and cliches about non-alignemnt and international peace reappeared, although some re-ordering of security priorities took place. In his first public speech as Prime Minister in June 1964, Lal Bahadur Shastri reiterated that non-alignment will continue to be "the fundamental basis of India's approach to world problems and her relations with other countries." He further said in London in December of that year that there was to be "no deviation" from the lines of policy laid down by his predecessor. We might at least understand these statements, even though we may disagree with them, if these lines of policy were clearly defined, but they were not. Surely, non-alignment could not simply mean the absence of formal treaties of alliances between India and other countries.

In all this rhetoric and debate about non-alignment and peace, India's leaders continue to underplay the fact that the world of the 1960s and 1970s has changed since the earlier days when India's international stance won her some accolades. Ever since the Cuban Missile Crisis of 1962, when the two super powers came face to face and, realizing the dangerous nuclear game they were playing, backed off, India's services either as a middleman or as a peacemaker have not been required. Today, the two super powers have more channels of communication open to one another than India with either of them. Consequently, India's foreign-policy-makers need to look at her priorities and commitments not only to assess today's world situation but also to prepare the nation for the future. In other words, India needs to concentrate on the problems nearer home, and we will discuss the policy of the smallest concentric circle in a later chapter.

B. INDO-U.S. RELATIONS

Beneath the clamour of contending ideologies, controversies regarding national policies, and approaches to mutual problems, the essential character of Indo-U.S. relations is rather simple and appears as a consistent and coherent pattern.

Historically the United States has pursued certain international interests[4] ever since its emergence as a nation-state. Until the Second World War, the American policy was directed primarily toward the nations of the Western hemisphere and Europe despite an occasional foray into Asian affairs. The aftermath of the Second World War brought about some fundamental and global changes in the traditional policies and attitudes of the United States. Two of the cardinal objectives of American foreign policy—predominance in the Western hemisphere and balance of power elsewhere—were shaken, and new approaches were necessary. This new situation also called for a change in the traditional American attitude of non-involvement in external affairs. Consequently, the formative years of America's foreign relations coincided with the emerging foreign policy of an independent India.

The initial years of Indo-U. S. relations were much like the newly-weds who settled down immediately to the serious task of learning about each other's attitudes, preferences, and desires without ever having the interlude of a honeymoon, not even a brief one. Naturally, there arose many misunderstadings followed by acrimonious arguments. The beginning of the Cold War in Europe, the American initiative for making military alliances and giving assistance, the emergance of Communism in China, the outbreak of the Korean conflict, etc. all were obstacles to an objective and natural evolution of relations between the two countries. A number of

American policy decisions were viewed with suspicion and alarm by the Government of India for their apparent reliance on military means for the resolution of international conflicts and for the corresponding de-emphasis on negotiated political settlements.

On the other hand, in the words of Prime Minister Nehru, India and the United States shared "a common faith in democratic institutions and the democratic way of life, and [were] dedicated to the cause of peace and freedom."[5] Nehru recognized that destiny had given the United States a major role in international affairs. He was anxious to see this tremendous power and responsibility utilized for maintaining peace and furthering human progress and freedom everywhere, for India's own continued progress heavily depended on achievement of these wider goals. But, in the heat of cold war passions, India's insistence upon a policy of non-alignment and peaceful settlement of disputes among nations was considerably misunderstood in the United States. Nehru talked about it in a radio broadcast on December 31, 1950, and said:

Today, if we talk of peace, sometimes people mistake it for appeasement of evil. The temper of peace is completely absent today and the only alternative to a surrender appears to many people to be war with all its terrible consequences. Surely, there are other alternatives which are far removed from surrender and yet lead to the objective aimed at. It is in this spirit that we have tried to approach the world's problems. We are not pacifists. We keep an army and a navy and air force and if danger threatens us we shall use them. But we seek no dominion over other people. Our sole object is to be left in peace ourselves to solve our own problems and, where possible, to help and cooperate with others. In doing so, we try not to be swept by passion and anger but to maintain the temper of peaceful approach.[6]

Unfortunately, neither America's policies nor attitudes appeared to harmonize with Nehru's views. The American policy under President Dwight D. Eisenhower and Secretary of State John Foster Dulles was not well disposed toward conciliation with adversaries or leaving the others alone. Dulles in particular pursued his anti-communism policy with an almost crusading zeal and relied primarily upon military responses.

Among the many areas of contention between India and the United States perhaps the single most important one turned out to be the two nation's divergent policies toward the Communist bloc nations, particularly the Soviet Union and Communist China. Many other differences are directly traceable to this primary issue. While the United States policy sought to contain the Soviet Union and China through a system of military alliances, India sought to promote a climate of peaceful coexistence and cooperation by recognizing the vital differences between their political and economic institutions and her own. It was toward this end that Nehru played a major role in bringing China into the Afro-Asian Conference at Bandung in 1955. He believed that containment or isolation of China was not only an unrealistic goal but actually harmful for the cause of peace, especially in Asia. Only this overriding policy goal can explain a number of previous Indian actions toward Chinese moves, such as Nehru's mild stand on the Chinese invasion of Tibet, India's peace efforts in Korea, which the United States viewed as showing undue warmth toward China, opposition to the United States sponsored "Uniting for Peace" resolution of November 1950, disassociation with the American move to brand China the aggressor in the Korean conflict, etc.

In view of the rather fundamental policy approaches between India and the United States regarding the two major communist nations, the Soviet Union and China, we can posit that, whenever relations between India and the Communists became cordial and mutually beneficial, the Indo-U.S. relation generally hit a low point. The Korean conflict of 1950-53, the highly popular Bulganin-Khrushchev visit to India in late 1955, among other events, illustrate this correlation. Of course, the most serious outcome of these policy differences turned out to be the American decision to arm Pakistan as a member of the Central and Southeast Asia Treaty Organization alliances. India's relations with the Soviet Union and even China in the 1950's were not hindered by any outstanding conflict of interests, territorial or otherwise, and relations could be based on an objective analysis of the conditions and a pragmatic approach to the problems. Relations with Pakistan, however, were an entirely different story. Since Indo-Pakistan relations are discussed in greater detail in a subsequent chapter, at this point, suffice it to say that American arms supply to Pakistan introduced a new and even a dangerous element into an

already tense situation between the two countries with an outstanding territorial dispute in Kashmir. India viewed the United
States' action as an endorsement of Pakistan's claims against her,
despite American assurances to the contrary.[7]

Indo-U.S. relations during the 1950s, in the main, remained
tense and were frequently marred by acrimony because neither
appreciated the other's policy goals. However, despite this
political climate the mutual involvement of the two countries in
economic, cultural, and educational areas continued to grow
during this time. The Eisenhower-Dulles policies came to a close
with the election of John F. Kennedy as President of the United
States, and a new American attitude and approach toward
India began to emerge. An inkling of this change appeared as
early as 1958 when Kennedy, then a Senator, remarked in a
speech on economic assistance to India:

If the Second Plan collapses, so may democratic India and
the democratic hope in all of Asia setting in motion forces which
would erode the broad security intersts of the United States
and its Allies. However sharply one may reject the concept of
American ideals impelling us to help others in need, however
blind one may be to the dependence of our economic well-being
upon closing the enormous prosperity gap between ourselves
and have-not nations, no thoughtful citizen can fail to see our
stake in the survival of a free government in India.[8]

In another speech on November 1, 1959 at Riverside, California,
John F. Kennedy talked about the momentous struggle between
India and China for the economic and political leadership of
Asia, "for the respect of all Asia, for the opportunity to demon-
strate whose way of life is the better." He left no doubt about his
sympathies when he said: "We want India to win that race with
Red China. We want India to be a free and thriving leader of a
free and thriving Asia."[9]

Kennedy showed an awareness and appreciation of political
realities in India and supported a number of India's policy
objectives. Again, in the Riverside speech, he emphasized that:
". . . if our interest [in supporting India] appears to be purely selfish,
anti-communist, and part of the Cold War—if it appears to the
Indian people that our motives are purely political—then we shall

play into the hands of Communist and Neutralist propagandists, cruelly distort America's image abroad, and undo much of the psychological effect that we expect from our generosity."[10]

This new American concern about India's problems was reflected in America's commitents for aid, which, in 1962 averaged some $740 million. In fact, with the exception of some $900 million allocated through PL-480 [the "Food for Peace" Act] in 1966, the Kennedy Administration's commitments were by far the largest of any since. Beginning in 1964, American policy under President Lyndon B. Johnson, with his preoccupation with Vietnam, started to drift away from India, and, by 1968, American aid to India had declined to a meagre $200 million a year.

The Kennedy Administration had some valuable opportunities to promote mutually beneficial policies and to reconstruct Indo-American relations on this basis. In 1962, when India faced China in a military confrontation along her Himalayan borders without meaningful support from any major power including the Soviet Union, the United States alone offered and supplied India with useful moral and material help. For a brief period, at least, it appeared that Indo-American relations might turn toward a joint concern about China. However, the brief Chinese military presence in Indian territory (beyond the disputed areas) and a reversal of Soviet stand, from a neutral/pro-Chinese stance to a neutral/ support India position, prompted India's policy-makers to exercise caution about too close an association with the United States. Furthermore, Russia's new support also permitted India to return to her fond policy of non-alignment; yet only a few weeks earlier, in its first vital test involving her real national interest, this same policy lay virtually shattered, and Nehru had then observed, "We were living in an artificial atmosphere of our own creation, and we have been shocked out of it."

Despite her ambivalent attitude toward a closer military association with the United States against China, India in 1963 asked the United States for a variety of advanced military hardware. This request received prolonged and serious consideration, but Washington finally rejected it late in 1964. Statements by Indian officials would lead one to believe that this decision was based upon a combination of vehement protests by America's ally, Pakistan, and her own reluctance to help India. The actual story, however, is much more involved and contained a variety of circumstantial and ideological components.

Perhaps the factor most important in preventing the development of an Indo-U.S. understanding regarding China was the tragic assassination of President Kennedy. His successor, Lyndon B. Johnson, was a politician of an entirely different mold' and lacked historical perspective on international events. He failed to appreciate the nature of the Chinese threat to India and its long-term implications for South Asian nations. Consequently, India's armament requests did not receive the priority treatment. During this same period (1962-64), the United States sought to promote the settlement of the Indo-Pakistani differences, particularly the Kashmir dispute, so that the two nations could develop a strategy of defence against China's expansionist policies in the region. The U.S. effort failed, however, as Pakistan's unwillingness to accept the partition of Kashmir along the cease-fire lines, with minor modifications, and India's rejection of Pakistan's proposal to divide the territory along communal lines (Kashmir Valley and the Hill Regions going to Pakistan and Ladakh and Jammu going to India) left the entire issue unresolved.

The death of Jawaharlal Nehru in May 1964, further weakened the chances for the development of a joint Indo-American position on the Indo-Pakistan dispute. At the time of Nehru's death, the Indian request for American arms was under high-level discussion, and Defence Minister Y. B. Chavan was in Washington discussing his long shopping list with American officials.

During my various conversations with both Indian and American officials during this period, one question persistently came up: "Can India, with her policy of non-alignment, realistically expect from either the Soviet Union or the United States their best weapons?" The underlying premise of the question was that neither the U.S. nor the U.S.S.R. could afford the risk that military secrets would be leaked to the other, and India surely needed the best in weapons and equipment if she did not want to experience another humiliation like the one in 1962. Although the American responses seemed deliberately vague and expressed the hope that "something might work out," Defence Minister Chavan was explicit and said: "The question of possible leakage of weapons' secrets has been seriously studied by Indian officials and adequate security measures have been taken. The

United States Government, to make sure that the weapons given to India did not get revealed to the U.S.S.R., sent a team of security officers to study and inspect the Indian arrangements in 1963. They returned and reported their findings to the U. S. authorities. On my visit [to Washington in 1964] I found a very encouraging response to our weapons' requests. Therefore, I presume the U.S. authorities found our precautions satisfactory."[11]

Despite this assessment, India's requests for weapons were turned down by the United States, and the reason for this refusal still remains unclear. If considerations of security were not a problem, as Defence Minister Chavan contended, what than? I believe that a simple and clear-cut answer to this question will not be available for some time to come. But, when one pieces all the evidence together, it is hard to escape the conclusion that India's insistence on maintaining the fictional framework of non-alignment, and thus her appearance of equating the prompt and genuine American concern for India after the Chinese attack in 1962 with the initially negative but subsequently modified Soviet response to the same situation, played a major role in America's decision.

The purpose of this discussion is not to bemoan a lost opportunity but more to draw attention to the misplaced priorities of policy-makers in India and their inability to adjust to new situations. I am not arguing that India should have rushed to form a military alliance with the United States and turned her back on the Soviet Union. What I am suggesting is that India's leaders ought to have explored every opportunity to arrive at a joint Indo-American approach toward China. After all, in the fast changing international situation since the Cuban Missile Crisis of 1962, neither alignment nor non-alignment has much relevance. What continues to be relevant, though, is a set of policy approaches to international problems, approaches based upon the interests of the nations involved. It was Nehru himself who once remarked. "This [non-alignment] in itself is not a policy." He considered non-alignment a means to secure and further India's "national interest."

In the aftermath of the India-China clash of 1962, India at first appeared ready to reconstruct her foreign policy in the context of her own national interests. As soon as the immediate Chinese military pressure eased, however, Nehru proceeded, not to explore ways to buttress India's interests, but instead to salvage the remains of an outdated and bankrupt policy. If the primary purpose of this return to non-alignment was to secure Soviet neutrality in conflicts where vital Indian interests might be involved, then this move was not only limited but short-sighted as well. The Soviet Union will pursue her policies, as always, according to her own well-defined interests ; and if and when Sino-Soviet differences are resolved, the Soviet Union will cease to support India's position against China. The Soviets have already taken a similar route regarding Indo-Pakistan differences over Kashmir, where from a decidedly pro-India stand they have moved toward a neutral position.

Beginning in 1965, the United States government under President Johnson became overwhelmingly involved in Vietnam and largely neglected events elsewhere in South Asia. At the time of the Indo-Pakistan conflict in September-October of 1965, the United States failed to honour the pledge given to India by President Eisenhower in 1954 and did not insist that Pakistan should stop using American equipment against India. Moreover, the U. S. suspended all supplies, including food and economic aid, to India, and this move was deeply resented throughout the country and further aggravated Indo-U. S. relations. The relations between 1966-68 were uneventful but generally at a low ebb.

Richard M. Nixon's inauguration as President of the United States in 1969 did not offer a promise of substantial change in Indo-U. S. relations. In a report to the United States Congress on February 18, 1970, President Nixon expressed the hope that "over the next decade India, Pakistan, and their friends have an opportunity to build substantially on the constructive elements . . . and, above all, to work together to avert further wasteful and dangerous conflict in the area."[12] Apart from generalities of this nature and a vague suggestion that the United States may provide "a shield if a nuclear power [presumably China] threatens the freedom . . .of a nation whose survival we consider vital to our security and the security of the region as a whole.[13] Conceivably, India under certain circumstances could qualify for American support if the United States made such a judgement, but the "Nixon Doctrine" does not contain any specific initiatives or overtures toward India. Under these conditions, it would be safe to assume that Indo-U. S. relations are likely to remain low-key for some time to come.

The United States' decision in October 1970, to sell arms to Pakistan as a one-time exception to the embargo on the sale of weapons to India and Pakistan, and the now famous tilt toward Pakistan during the 1971 Indo-Pakistan war, once again created popular skepticism of American intentions in the region. The Government and people of India have remained dissatisfied with the American explanations, both about the arms supply and the tilt toward Pakistan ; and it appears that, if some serious and genuine efforts are not soon undertaken to clear the air, Indo-U. S. relations may continue to remain severely strained.

C. INDO-SOVIET RELATIONS

In his first statement of policy, Nehru referred to future relations with the Soviet Union by saying : "To that other great nation of the modern world, the Soviet Union, which also carries a vast responsibility for shaping world events, we send our greetings. They are our neighbours in Asia, and inevitably we shall have to undertake many common tasks and have much to do with each other."[14]

However, it takes two to undertake common tasks. The Soviet Union under Joseph Stalin was guided by doctrinaire interpretations of the prevalent international situation. The Secretary of the Soviet Communist Party, Andire Zhdanov, was expounding the theme that bourgeois national movements, such as the Indian National Movement, were frauds and that they served the interests of British and American imperialism. In his view, the world was divided into two camps—the imperialistic and anti-democratic camp led by the Western powers and the anti-imperialistic and democratic camp headed by the Soviet Union. Since India was not a member of the Soviet-headed camp, it was obvious to Zhdanov that she was still enslaved by the imperialists and was obedient to them.[15]

This attitude notwithstanding, the official U. S. S. R. policy toward free India was not hostile or belligerent but merely indifferent. The Soviets, at the time, were too deeply involved in European affairs and did not possess sufficient resources to divert their attention to many parts of the world. India was a Soviet neighbour in geographical terms only, and did not share any common cultural, economic, or historical bonds. Even though diplomatic relations between the two countries were established promptly upon India's independence, the diplomatic activity remained low.

In the midst of these inopportune conditions, the Soviet diplomats in India were further constricted by their preoccupation with the doctrine and made little effort to find out whether Indian independence was a fraud or a reality. This attitude of treating India as an Anglo-American colony belied all objective observations, but Soviet leaders, Communist theoreticians and a number of their Indian apologists kept the theme up for five long years.

State relations between India and the Soviet Union began to show some improvement during the Korean conflict of 1950-53. India's differing stands on various issues during this period, such as her opposition to the U.S.-sponsored resolution to brand China as an aggressor, Nehru's call to the United Nations forces not to cross the 38th parallel, and India's position on the prisoners of war issue made an impact on Soviet policy-makers. This new appreciation of India was first reflected when Joseph Stalin received the Indian Ambassador, Madame Vijaya Lakshmi Pandit, Nehru's sister, in 1950, for the first time. Madame Pandit's successor to Moscow, S. Radhakrishnan, was shown far greater warmth and respect by Soviet leaders and was received by Stalin on several occassions.

It appears that the Soviet leaders had not yet clearly made up their minds as to what direction to pursue in their dealings with India. While Stalin in 1952 informed Radhakrishnan of his appreciation for India's policy of settling international disputes through peaceful negotiations, his representative at the United Nations, A. Vyshinsky, in December of the same year, characterized India's stand on the Korean prisoners of war issue thus : "At best you are dreamers and idealists, at worst you don't understand your own position, and camouflage horrible American policy."[16] *This one step forward and two steps backward* Soviet style in her relations with India lingerd on until Stalin's death in 1953. New Soviet leaders were emerging and dramatic changes were forthcoming.

The year 1953 constitutes a decisive watershed in Soviet policy toward India. The ideological determinants of the Stalin era were being de-emphasized, and changing domestic and external enrivonmental factors began to play a perceptible role in Soviet international behaviour. Whatever may have been their initial intentions,

the Soviet leaders' new stance toward India showed an acute awareness of the fast moving changes in the South Asian region. Until
1953, Soviet policy had accomplished little, in contrast to the
impressive diplomatic and political gains made by the United
States as well as China. Consequently, the Soviet leaders started
to respond rationally to developments in India. Nehru was no longer considered a lackey of the imperialists, but a respected nationalist leader and a spokesman of the peace-loving emerging nations.
In this context, the Soviets also departed from the earlier Zhdanov
thesis of a simply bifurcated world to the image of a troika.

The neutral bloc, described as a "zone of peace," was seen as
a potential ally of the Soviet bloc in a loose coalition against the
West under the broad rubric of "peace and anti-imperalism."
The obverse side of this alliance, of course, was the further post-
ponement of a revolutionary programme in favour of a prolonged
collaboration with the "bourgeois nationalist" programme.[17]

In India, the new orienation in Soviet policy was designed to
strengthen Nehru's policy of non-alignment, a move prompted not
only by the type of appraisal discussed above, but also by the
emergence of China as Soviet Russia's future formidable rival.
Georgi M. Malenkov's statements in August 1953, that "the
position of so large a state as India is of great importance for
strengthening peace in the East" and that India had made "a
considerable contribution to the efforts of the peace-loving countries aimed at ending the war in Korea"[18] were a recognition of
India's new international position. This new awareness soon
became multi-faceted and a great deal of Indo-Soviet activity in
the cultural social, and economic fields began to occur.

As noted above, the changed Soviet stance toward India was
prompted by a number of considerations, including the rise of
China as a potential Soviet rival in Asia. The importance of this
last factor—the Sino-Soviet rivalry—has not been given due credit
in most studies on Indo-Soviet relations. I believe that a brief
discussion will bring us closer to a more rational and accurate
understanding of the vital national interest component of Soviet
policy in India. Inversely, it should also help us to analyze the
structure of Indian policy and its lack of a conscious pursuit of
any well-defined national objectives. One may even go so far as
to say that Indian policy-makers were probably totally unaware
of Soviet calculations at the time.

Soviet relations with China have been uneasy for a long time. With the public exchange of charges and counter-charges in the early 1960s, this fact is now a public knowledge. However, there is reason to believe that the Soviets had misgivings about the victory of Mao Tse-tung's movement from the very beginning. Certainly, there has been little historic friendship between the Russians and the Chinese, and some of Stalin's earlier policies of giving the nascent Chinese communists inappropriate advice for revolutionary activity in a peasant-dominated country as well as his cooperation with the Kuomintang promised to cause difficulties in future relations. The recent history of the Sino-Soviet schism is well known, but bits and pieces of public evidence of earlier discords have now become available. C. L. Sulzberger of the *New York Times* described how early in 1950, prior to the outbreak of the Korean War, an important Russian had suggested to him "that Washington and Moscow should jointly elaborate some kind of Chinese outlook;" he added that "Russia alone cannot handle the problem of China. It is a thirty-years' task for America and Russia together." Pursuing this line even during the Korean War, the same official, meeting with an American diplomat of some rank "confided that Moscow was not getting on well with Peking and the economic burden of aiding China was immense."[19]

In 1953, the Soviet leaders appeared incapable of participating decisively in the settlement of the Korean War, when the Chinese representatives at Panmunjom insisted that the Soviet Union could participate only as an observer. As the 1950's drew to a close, the Sino-Soviet relations worsened appreciably. The withdrawal of Soviet technicians and advisors from China, far from discouraging the Chinese, proved largelly ineffective and made China more defiant. Despite the sobering counsel of numerous Chinese leaders who recognized the need for Soviet military assistance as the only means for keeping the Chinese army viable, the xenophobes among them were happy to dispense with the services of the Soviet experts, who were considered to be agents of Soviet influence in China.

The fundamental reasons for China's independence within the Communist world are not too difficult to ascertain, but Chinese nationalism and an independent Chinese Communist Party were perhaps the two most important reasons. Unlike the communist parties in Eastern Europe, the Chinese Communist Party was never dominated by the Soviet Union, and even through the 1950s, when it appeared to adhere to Moscow idealogically, it was always independent as an organization. So when the Chinese decided to operate alone, the Soviet Union was powerless to intervene in the classical style and devoted its energies to more traditional goals of politics through tried and proven instruments of statecraft. The Soviet Union decided to launch her diplomatic offensive in other countries of Asia and focussed primarily on India with a view to promoting a counter-force to the growing power and influence of China. In essance, therefore, the dramatic convergence of Indian and Soviet views on international events in later years was by no means accidental. It was brought about by a deliberate and conscious Soviet effort. To answer the question, "Who benefited most in this arrangement?" We need to examine the balance sheet of the Indo-Soviet merger in terms of their long-term interests, and we must not get sidetracked into a debate about rubles and kopecks or praise and plaudits.

The decade from 1955-65 can be described as the most cordial and mutually beneficial period in Indo-Soviet relations. The two nations appeared to be largely in agreement on all major international issues and strongly supported each other's particular national interests. Also, by 1955, both countries had formulated clear and positive policies toward specific problems, although some change was perceptible somewhat earlier. The balance sheet of Indo-Soviet relations during this decade clearly runs in India's favour. Apart from the substantial economic benefits, the Soviet's political and diplomatic support of India remained strong and apparently was much needed in this period. Of course, this trend was greatly facilitated by the actions of other powers, especially the United States' support of Pakistan's position on Kashmir, the U. S.'s military assistance to Pakistan, and developments in China.

The Khrushchev-Bulganin statements during their visit to India in late 1955, left no doubt regarding Soviet Union's conscious decision to build her South Asia policy around India. Soviet support of India's position in Kashmir, Khrushchev's call for the liquidation of the Portuguese colonies in India, and the Soviet endorsement of Nehru's policy of non-alignment all were positive gains for India. In return, it would appear, the Soviet Union received little at the time except appreciation and praise. But since the Soviet Union had foreseen future difficulties with China, she was perfectly willing to collect her debts from India at a later date. In other words, the Soviet policy toward India in 1955 was consciously designed to promote a wedge between India and China in order to relieve the growing Chinese pressure upon them to a certain extent. In *realpolitik* terms, we can contend that Indian policy-makers failed to see this Soviet manoeuvre at the time and drifted unknowingly into an anti-China stance. If, however, India's decision was conscious, then it raises a host of new questions regarding the country's foreign policy objectives and priorities. But as the events of 1962 indicated, India's decision was not deliberate. Therefore, the question still remains: Why? Was Nehru unable to understand the nature of the developments or was the policy and decision-making apparatus of the Indian government inadequate? Suffice it to say that the importance of this drift in Indian policy was not lost on the Chinese leaders. In 1959 they datelined India's "deviation from progressive policies from the latter half of 1956"[20] and initiated their own counter moves against India on several fronts including her borders.

The convergence of Indo-Soviet views on anti-imperialism further facilitated cooperation among the two countries in the international arena. India, as an influential member of the emerging Afro-Asian bloc of nations, received considerable attention from Soviet leaders both in bilateral dealings and at the United Nations. Nehru's strong denunciation of the Anglo-French-Israeli action against Egypt in 1956, his condemnation of the Belgian intervention in the Congo in 1960, and his censure of the American support of the "Bay of Pigs" incident involving Cuba in 1961, all coincided with the Soviet's position on these issues. Conversely, India's mild criticism of the Soviet action in Hungary in 1956 appeared to be designed not to offend that nation. Consequently, the Western powers accused India's leaders of employing double standards in judging Soviet and Western actions. The Indian leaders, however, maintained that the Western powers during this period deserved a larger share of the blame for these events and for accentuating tensions in the world.

It would seem that Indian leaders were ostensibly guilty of a double standard of judgement, but the reasons for this phenomenon need to be explored to gain a proper perspective. First of all, the Western powers had a long and disgraceful record of colonial subjugation and exploitation. Even though the United States did not belong to this category, her support of the other Western colonial powers on many occasions made her word suspect in India. The Soviet Union, on the other hand, even though her borders contained large numbers of non-white peoples, was not viewed as a colonial power in the traditional sense of the word. The Russian state since the Soviet takeover in 1917 had actually become a bit smaller after adjustments, regarding Finland, Poland, and later China, were made. In other words, in India the heterogenous ethnic character of the Soviet Union was viewed as nothing more than a demographic expansion of the Russian-speaking people, a move much like the expansion of English-Speaking Americans in the United States from the Atlantic to the Pacific Oceans.

Secondly, India's leaders viewed the Western nations' system of military alliances with their hundreds of bases encircling the Communist countries as a major cause of tension in the world, and a number of Soviet actions were consequently treated as defensive reactions to the original provocation and danger.

Finally, Indo-Soviet relations were generally free of national irritants arising out of territorial, economic, or historical factors. By contrast, India's dealings with other Western nations included a number of unresolved issues that prevented the growth of cordial relations. Western support of Portuguese colonial holdings in India, the discriminatory treatment of people of Indian origin in many British-controlled territories in Africa, and Anglo-American support of Pakistani claims in Kashmir, among others, were some of these sensitive issues. The 1955-65 decade of Indo-Soviet relations turned out to be a remarkable feat of Soviet diplomacy. India made some limited gains regarding Kashmir and Goa, but the long-term advantages accrued to the Soviet Union, whose leaders were successful in relieving China's pressure upon them but without supporting the Indian position on China.

Premier Nikita S. Khrushchev in his report to the U.S.S.R. Supreme Soviet on December 12, 1962, did not support the Indian position on the Indo-Chinese border. His statement expressed the hope that the governments of the two countries would not allow tensions to rise any further and would settle the dispute with due consideration for their mutual interests and in the spirit of the traditional friendship between the peoples of China and India. His stand was basically neutral: "It is especially painful to us that there has been shed the blood of the sons of the fraternal People's Republic of China and our friend, the Republic of India." "We trust in the wisdom of the leaders of China and India, and hope that they . . . will ensure a reasonable resolution of the conflict." "We ardently wish to see the two great powers . . . fully restore and consolidate their ancient traditional friendship."[21]

As is generally true with neutral positions, this particular Soviet stand did not endear the Russians to either India or China. The Indians expressed great disappointment, while the Chinese received the Soviet statement with derision and contempt and went on to say that the Russian position confirmed China's earlier fears of Soviet collusion with the imperialist and bourgeois powers against the People's Republic of China.

While the Soviets hesitated, the United States and the United Kingdom reacted favourably to India's requests for armaments and promptly started their delivery. The extent of the impact of the Anglo-American action upon the Soviet's re-evaluation of their earlier stand is not clear, but we can infer that this development, coupled with the derisive Chinese reactions, played an important role in the Soviet decision to supply India with armaments. Some have viewed this decision as a personal triumph for Nehru's diplomacy, but we must not forget that the Chinese reaction made it possible. It appears that the Chinese demanded complete Soviet support of their position against India as the price for an accommodation with the Soviets, and this fidelity, of course, would have required that the Soviets abandon their friendship with India. The far-reaching consequences for their position in the region made this alternative clearly unacceptable. Furthermore, a pro-Chinese Soviet stand would have greatly encouraged a pro-Western sentiment in India and could even have brought about an Indo-American military arrangement against China. Consequently, after calculating the relative gains and losses of a doubtful accommodation with a powerful and rival neighbour (China), in contrast to the definite political gains to be made in India, the Soviet Union decided to give military support to India. That the Soviet Union did not endorse India's position regarding the disputed areas gives further credence to the assumption that her military assistance to India was more of a counter move to check India's drift toward the United States than support against China. In other words, the Soviet Union preferred to keep India non-aligned and influence her policies in this framework than to see India develop a pro-Western outlook in world affairs.

An analysis of these developments, especially in the light of subsequent events such as the Indo-Pakistan conflict over Kashmir in 1965, leads me to conclude that the Soviet reversal was not really a triumph for Indian diplomacy and that the actual gains were reaped by the Soviet Union. The Soviet Union came through virtually unscathed in this event and was successful in preventing the growth of an Anglo-American influence in India. She did not support India's claims against China and thus provided for a reconciliation with China at an opportune moment. In any event, the Chinese had already occupied the territories they claimed, and the Indians, with or without Soviet assistance, are not likely to regain them either through force or through negotiations.

With the death of Nehru in May and the ouster of Khrushchev in October 1964, the decade of post-Stalin Indo-Soviet relations came to a close. During this period the two countries had cooperated extensively in many areas. Despite a number of disagreements in their outlook on international events, such as Hungary, the Congo episode, and Khrushchev's call for a "troika" arrangement in the United Nations, their bilateral relations grew steadily. For example, the Indo-Soviet trade grew steadily : At the beginning of 1953, India's trade with the Soviet Union was barely one per cent of her total foreign trade. In 1964 this percentage had risen to sixteen and the Soviet Union had acquired third place among India's trading partners.

With the loss of the two principal architects of friendly Indo-Soviet relations, Nehru and Khrushchev, and the assumption of power by Brezhnev-Kosygin in the Soviet Union, and Lal Bahadur Shastri in India, a new situation began to emerge. The Indian leaders appeared eager to maintain the established relationship, but the Soviet leaders did not wish to continue the *status quo* for a number of reasons.

Apart from the changed position of the Soviet Union generally throughout the world, perhaps the most obvious imbalance to Brezhnev-Kosygin appeared to be in their relations with China and Pakistan. The structure of Indo-Soviet relations had much to do with this state of affairs, and they concluded that Khrushchev had overcommitted the Soviet Union in favour of India in both the Indo-Pakistan and Sino-Indian disputes. From the increased tempo of Sino-Soviet dialogue during this period, Chou En-lai's visit to Moscow in November 1964, and Kosygin's two visits to Peking during 1965, it is evident that the new team in Moscow was seriously exploring an accommodation with China. That these efforts at the time did not produce the desired results regarding China, however, did not mean that Indo-Soviet relations could continue as usual. Unlike Khrushchev, the new leaders were more pragmatic and expected a *quid pro quo* basis for their dealings with India ; and since India was both unable and unwilling to endorse the Soviet stand on any and all issues, ralations between the two countries entered a new phase.

The first indications of a change in Soviet policy regarding Kashmir appeared when Ayub Khan, after being President for nearly seven years, visited the Soviet Union for the first time in April 1965. Unlike the preceding years when the Soviets considered Kashmir as part of India and a closed topic not subject to discussion, the Kashmir issue was discussed this time.[22] Even though the official communique did not specifically refer to the Kashmir problem, President Ayub Khan's impression of a Soviet policy change toward India was later proved accurate. Both during the Rann of Kutch conflict in April and the Indo-Pakistan war over Kashmir in September 1965, the Soviet Union expressed neutrality toward the two warring countries. The Tashkent Declaration of January 10, 1966, symbolically confirmed the new Soviet position in South Asia whereby the Kremlin elevated itself to the role of a statesman deeply concerned for the cause of peace between India and Pakistan. This new posture, needless to say, could not permit the Soviet leaders to take sides on issues dividing the two countries, and therefore the Kashmir issue, once again, became negotiable. Article I of the Tashkent Declaration said in part:

They [The Prime Minister of India and the President of Pakistan] considered that the interests of peace in their region. . . were not served by the continuance of tension between the two countries. It was against this background that Jammu and Kashmir was discussed, and each of the sides set forth its respective position.[23]

This new Soviet role, no doubt, was partly in response to the Chinese activities in Pakistan, but its main thrust was aimed at replacing the American position in the region. The United States with its preoccupation with Vietnam did not even attempt to counter the Russian move. It appears that, beginning with Tashkent, the long-range objectives of the two super powers in South Asia started to converge, and the Soviet Union, like the United States, has become a *status quo* power. The Soviet Union is now interested primarily in maintaining a peaceful and secure southern flank, a position made explicit in an officially-inspired commentary in *Pravda* during the Indo-Pakistan fighting in 1965 : "...Strengthening the ties between the U. S. S. R. and Pakistan must be regarded as a part of a general policy aimed at ensuring peace in Asia and throughout the World. We would like Soviet-Pakistani relations, like our traditional friendship with India, to be a stablizing factor in the situation in Asia and to contribute to the normalization of relations between Pakistan and India."[24]

The continued Soviet economic assistance to both India and Pakistan, and the dependence of the recipients on such help, have made this new Soviet role a viable concern. Indo-Soviet relations in the 1970's, despite the Indo-Soviet Treaty of Peace, Friendship and Cooperation of August 1971, do not bear a special relationship and it will be well for India to take account of the new situation and to reformulate her own foreign policy objectives in terms of her own priorities and resources.

NOTES

[1] K. P. S. Menon, "Nehru's Foreign Policy," *The Hindustan Times*, May 27, 1965, p. 1.
[2] For a detailed discussion of American policy in South Asia, see : Norman W. Brown, *The United States and India and Pakistan* (Cambridge, Mass. : Harvard University Press, 1963);Norman D. Palmer, *South Asia and the United States Policy* (Boston, Mass. : Houghton Mifflin Company, 1966); and Baljit Singh, "The United States and the India-Pakistan Conflict," *Parliamentary Studies*, Vol. 9, No. 12 (December, 1965), pp. 15-19. For Soviet policy, see : Arthur Stein, *India and the Soviet Union* (Chicago: University of Chicago Press, 1969); J. A. Naik, *Soviet Policy Toward India – From Stalin to Brezhnev* (Delhi : Vikas Publications, (1970); Mohammad Ayub Kahn, *Pakistan Perspective* (Washington, D. C.: Embassy of Pakistan, 1965); V. V. Balabushevich and Bimal Prasad (eds.), *India and the Soviet Union* (Delhi : Peoples Publishing House, 1969); and Sangat Singh, *Pakistan's Foreign Policy* (New York: Asia Publishing House,

1970).

[3] Jawaharlal Nehru, *India's Foreign Policy*, p. 70.

[4] For a detailed interpretation of American foreign policy objectives see : Hans J. Morgenthau, "The American Tradition in Foreign Policy," in Roy C. Macridis (ed.), *Foreign Policy in World Politics*, Second Edition (Englewood Cliffs, N. J.: Prentice Hall, Inc., 1962), pp. 201-224.

[5] Jawaharlal Nehru on World Affairs—1946-64, *Foreign Affairs Reports*, Vol. XIII, No. 6 (Special Issue) (June, 1964), p. 81.

[6] *Ibid.*, p. 84.

[7] For American assurances to India after her decision to arm Pakistan, see President Eisenhower's letter to Prime Minister Nehru in Peter U. Carl (ed.), *Documents on American Foreign Relations, 1954* (New York : Harper, 1955), pp. 374-375.

[8] John F. Kennedy, *The Strategy of Peace* (Ed. Allan Nevins) (New York: Popular Library, 1961), p. 183.

[9] *Ibid.*, pp. 178-179.

[10] *Ibid.*, p. 179.

[11] Remarks made in a personal interview with Author in New Delhi, June 1964.

[12] Richard M. Nixon, *U. S. Foreign Policy for the 1970's: A New Strategy for Peace* (Washington, D. C. : No Publisher), 1970, p. 59.

[13] *Ibid.*, p. 55.

[14] Radio Broadcast from New Delhi, September 7, 1946. cf. "Jawaharlal Nehru on World Affairs—1946-64," p. 76.

[15] For full text of Zhdanov thesis, see : *Pravda*, October 22, 1947. This is a long statement and primarily concerns itself with the division of the world into two camps. References to India are incidental and are used to illustrate the main thesis. But the statement is very important in terms of the Soviet view of Indian independence movement and their lack of appreciation of Indian leaders.

[16] Quoted in *The Times of India*, December 3, 1952.

[17] Marshall D. Shulman, *Stalin's Foreign Policy Reappraised* (Cambridge, Mass.: Harvard University Press, 1963), p. 263.

[18] *Current Digest of Soviet Press*, September 5, 1953.

[19] C. L. Sulzberger, *The New York Times*, February 10, 1967. The procedure used in this exchange is quite innovative. Soviet leaders have often found newspapermen suitable for diplomatic contacts, for not only were they ex-officio to decision-making, but often the leadership of the Soviet Union and that of other nations could by-pass the bureaucracies that would have been involved during a formal diplomatic interchange.

[20] Bhabani Sen Gupta, *The Fulcrum of Asia* (New York: Pegasus, 1970) p. 76.

[21] N. S. Khrushchev, "The Present International Situation and the Foreign Policy of the Soviet Union," *Documents of Current History, No. 27*, (New York: Crosscurrents Press, 1963), pp. 39-44.

[22] Ayub Khan, *Friends Not Masters* (London: Oxford University Press, 1967), pp. 168-174.

[23] The *Tashkent Declaration* (New Delhi: Publications Division, Government of India, 1966), p. 1.

[24] Quoted in Naik, *op. cit.*, p. 138.

CHAPTER IV

INDIA AND THE THIRD WORLD

A. HISTORICAL BACKGROUND

INDIA'S HISTORY HAS been one of a continuous and successive infusion of ideas and cultures from other lands. The Aryans, Greeks, Sakas, Huns, Moguls, and Arabs, to mention a few, all migrated to India, were absorbed into the culture of the subcontinent, and thereby added to the intellectual richness and social complexity of Indian life.[1] Despite the long period of British domination during which the Indian polity and society remained dormant and stood isolated from the Afro-Asian world, the essential blends of different strains and elements survived. Censequently, a sense of unity in diversity continues to serve as the basis of India's outlook, both at home and abroad.

Although India is an ancient country, she is still young in the context of her role in foreign affairs. At the time of her independence, the policy statements alluding to her historic ties with the emerging nations were more in the nature of certain theoretical propositions than specific policies, which were yet to develop. Despite an undercurrent of Asian and, later on, Afro-Asian unity and outlook, the two hundred years of Western colonial and imperialist domination had produced great economic, social, political, and psychological obstacles to their realization. Perhaps the most notable consequence of foreign rule in Asia and Africa was the isolation of these countries from each other and their orientation toward the ruling metropolitan power. The ancient routes through which trade and ideas had travelled in the past ceased to function and the colonies began to look out across the oceans to one European colonial power or other for matters ranging from economics to culture. The task of rebuilding pre-colonial ties, therefore, was more of an emotional response to a new situation which was developing in Asia at the time rather than a well-defined and systematic plan of action. Nehru's comment— ''For too long have we of Asia been petitioners in

Western Courts and Chancelleries. That story must now belong to the past.''[2]—was merely an expression and a hope.

During the long Indian renaissance beginning in the nineteenth century when nationalism led to national independence in 1947, one is hard pressed to find any meaningful evidence supporting a Pan-Asian or Afro-Asian awareness among the Indian leaders. The Indian nationalism was directly stimulated by the British, who posed a serious threat to the nation's traditions, culture, religion, and social order. Unlike the earlier invaders, the British were not only completely alien but also technologically superior. Moreover, through the political unification, administrative centralization, modernization of the armed forces, introduction of English as the official language, development of transportation and communication systems, and the promotion of a "national economy," to supersede the traditional economics of "village self-sufficiency," the British were the first invaders who systematically promoted the transformation of the country. The British challenge, therefore, was deep, abiding, and multi-faceted and needed to be taken seriously. Despite its exploitative character, British rule provided a degree of stimulation that resulted in social, economic, and political gains and led to India's eventual liberation from that very rule.

Indian renaissance can be traced to a series of social reform movements starting in Bengal, the region that had first felt the impact of the British. Beginning with Raja Rammohan Roy and his Brahmo Samaj in 1828, a whole series of movements began in various parts of the country. Most of these movements recognized the necessity of reform and change within Indian society and polity if they were to succeed against alien encroachment. That these efforts were quite successful can be seen by the fact that after a vigorous missionary activity for over a century, Chirstians in India did not account for even two per cent of the population at the time the British departed in 1947.

The social reform movements generated considerable intellectual ferment and set the stage for a political awakening. Ironically, an Englishman, Allan Octavian Hume, led the way when he founded the Indian National Congress in 1885. A long line of distinguished men provided leadership to the political movement during the next sixty years of struggle. The point to remember, however, is that, with rare exceptions, their outlook was over-whelmingly national. They did not project their national struggle as part of a Pan-Asian or Afro-Asian movement against colonial domination. India's involvement in the affairs of the Third-world nations is a recent development. It gained momentum only after India herself became independent. Furthermore, in Nehru's world view, India needed to play a prominent role in the area. Consequently, India's relations with the emerging nations must be viewed as such and not necessarily an outgrowth of some historical relationships. Of course, the common bond of anti-colonialism and anti-imperialism greatly facilitated the development of common approaches to international problems and provided a much needed ideological cement to the nascent movement.

The late Achmed Sukarno of Indonesia once expressed this drive for national self-determination in the following manner:

We mean that all nations must become independent. All nations must have the freedom to be free, the freedom to arrange their own national life in accordance with their own wishes, the freedom to be free to build their own foundation— politically, economically, culturally. We mean that all nations must be free to arrange their international relations as they see fit, based on the principle of equality, justice and mutual bene- fit. We mean that no power shall interfere in the struggle of any other nation to find its own national concept, that no power shall attempt to force any other nation to change its ideology.[3]

Sukarno's statement succinctly expresses what Nehru had often said was the basis of India's relations with other nations. Sukarno's words emphasize the great similarity in outlook among the leaders of the emerging nations, a similarity that began with the Asian Relations Conference held in New Delhi in 1947. At this conference, one of the resolutions passed condemned the Dutch military attack on Indonesia.

Perhaps the most well-known and well-publicized major con- ference of the Afro-Asian nations was held in Bandung, Indo- nesia, in April 1955. The main purpose of that conference was to promote and consolidate economic, cultural, and political cooperation between the nations of Asia and Africa and to pursue a common policy against imperialism and colonialism in all its manifestations. In essence, then, India's relations with the

Third World were organized in this general framework of anti-colonialism to promote mutually beneficial contacts. Naturally, among this vast group of nations called the Third World, relations were closer and more meaningful among a few nations than the remaining many. Apart from other factors, the most important element in the development of this special relationship among a small number of these countries was a certain trust and comradeship between the leaders. Nehru, Sukarno, Nasser, Nkrumah, and Tito had become extremely close and cordial; and as a result, relations between India, Indonesia, Egypt, Ghana, and Yugoslavia were marked by a fraternal aura in whatever joint ventures these nations engaged themselves.

A discussion of India's relations with the entire membership of the Third World nations, in my view, is not only unnecessary but not likely to illustrate India's policy any more significantly or fully than can be accomplished through a selective presentation. I will, therefore, discuss in some detail only two policy areas: (1) Southeast Asia and (2) West Asia.

In Southeast Asia, I will focus upon India's policy in Vietnam, to illustrate an area of general concern to India but one where no special interests or factors were involved.

In discussing West Asia, I will attempt to illustrate a different aspect of Indian policy. Not only are the Arab World and India closer to each other in historical, cultural, and economic terms, but also the existence of a close personal relationship between Nehru and Nasser gave India's Arab policy a new dimension.

In passing, let me just say that India's relations with the emerging nations in Latin America and Sub-Saharan Africa are more or less routine except for an occasional spark here and there, namely, the apartheid in the Union of South Africa. The level of contact is rather low, and no urgent matters of conflict or cooperation engage the attention of India's decision-makers. In a way, this entire area receives almost no systematic attention. Indeed, it may be more accurate to say that, for reasons of non-policy, it is hard to discuss India's role in this large and potentially critical part of the world.

B. INDIA'S POLICY AND THE VIETNAM CONFLICT

As indicated earlier, one of the primary purposes of a foreign policy is to influence the behaviour of other states. This intended objective may be accomplished by a variety of tools that are available to foreign policy decision-makers, including diplomacy, coercion, trade and aid, propaganda, infiltration and subversion, and moral persuasion. India has sought to employ moral persuasion as its main weapon to influence the developments in Vietnam,

The reasons for this attitude of Indian leaders have been ably discussed elsewhere and need not be reviewed here.[4] Reference must, however, be made to the belief held by Mr. Nehru that India's policy of non-alignment pursued within the context of Panchsheel[5] lessened tensions in the world, enlarged the "area of peace," promoted reciprocal confidence among nations and paved the way for greater international cooperation. These developments w ere viewed as conducive to seeking peaceful solutions of international questions through methods of negotiation and conciliation.

When I examine Indian foreign policy regarding Vietnam, I find that it has been designed to promote the following three objectives:

1. National self-determination;
2. A negotiated settlement of the conflict; and
3. Non-intervention by other nations in Vietnamese affairs.

Generally speaking, those objectives have been India's policy toward Vietnam for the past nineteen years. Prime Minister Nehru made somewhat similar suggestions to the Geneva Conference on Indo-China in 1954.[6] When the "Geneva Agreement on the Cessation of Hostilities in Vietnam" was signed in July 1954, India was selected to act as chairman of the three-nation (India, Canada, and Poland) "International Commission for Supervision and Control" (ICSC), established under the agreements. The main purpose of the ICSC, of course, was to see that the agreements were fully implemented. Consequently, the substance of India's policy toward Vietnam during the period of 1954-62 was expressed as the desire to implement the Geneva agreements and was conducted through the chairmanship of the ICSC for Vietnam.

On October 17, 1954, President Ho Chi Minh assured the

Indian Prime Minister "that he was giving and would continue to give his full cooperation to the International Conmission to implement the Agreements." Furthermore, "He was anxious to solve all remaining problems peacefully and cooperatively so that the countries of Indo-China may live independently and prosper without any external interference."[7]

Again, on April 10, 1955, Mr. Nehru and Mr. Pham Van Dong, then Deputy Prime Minister and Foreign Minister of North Vietnam, in a joint statement, expressed the hope that the Geneva Agreements would be implemented "both in their terms and spirit. They were in agreement on the importance of free elections and the achievement of unity of Vietnam as provided for by the Geneva Agreements."[8]

General elections were to have taken place in July, 1956, that is, two years from the date of the agreements, and were to be held "under the supervision of an international commission composed of the member states of the International Commission for Supervision and Control."[9] The General elections, however, did not take place, and the character of the Vietnam situation from 1956 on began to change qualitatively. Consequently, the role of the ICSC also underwent a transformation.[10] From a body that was designed to oversee the implementation of certain agreements; the ICSC rapidly became an agency in charge of receiving complaints and passing often meaningless and unenforceable rules. The story of the failures and frustrations of the International Commission is well known and need not be discussed here.[11] What is significant, however, is the change in India's outlook toward the ICSC, a change that became evident around 1959.

During the five-year period between 1954-1959, a great deal had taken place both in South and North Vietnam and in and around India. By this time, in contrast to earlier doubts, the total Communist character of the Ho Chi Minh regime had been fully established. The question of the re-unification of Vietnam turned out to be more complex than the Government of India had earlier thought it was; there was the moral problem of whether the people of South Vietnam had a right to have the government of their choice. Furthermore, the aggressive activities of the Communists in and around India alarmed Mr. Nehru, and he began to have second thoughts about the desirability of a unified Vietnam that would extend the Communist's influence and power deep into South and Southeast Asia. This position, of course, in the absence of any documentation, is nothing more than an inference based upon circumstantial evidence.

Nevertheless India's position in the ICSC changed on a number of key matters. The first indication of this new policy came in 1959 when the ICSC, over the objections of the Polish representative, referred to the problem of North Vietnam's subversive activities in South Vietnam.[12] During the same year the ICSC, with the Polish member again dissenting, did not consider the increase in military personnel of the United States Military Advisory Group a violation of the Geneva Agreements. These decisions by the ICSC invoked protests by the North Vietnamese government, which called them "unjust" and remarked that the ICSC's rulings were introducing obstacles to the implementation of the Geneva Agreements; moreover, said the North Vietnamese it was "clearly evident that such decisions provide favourable conditions for the United States imperialists to intensify their interference in South Vietnam, thus further endangering the security of the Democratic Republic of Vietnam as well as peace in Indo-China and Southeast Asia."[13]

By 1962 the Vietnam situation had changed radically, and any expectations of solving the conflict within the provisions of the Geneva Agreements were unrealistic. The intensification of the civil war in the country due to North Vietnam's increased support of the Viet Cong and the ever-increasing United States support of the successive regimes in the South magnified the problem into a big-power confrontation.

As far as the Soviet Union and Communist China were concerned, this East-West confrontation was still indirect, but the danger of its becoming a direct conflict was ever present.

In these changed circumstances, India proposed that the concerned parties review the entire Vietnamese situation afresh and strive for a negotiated settlement. The consequences of an extending and escalating war in Vietnam have been patently obvious to all concerned, and India was no exception. Deeply preoccupied with her own domestic and foreign problems, India found it impossible to do more than, once again, extend her good offices to the warring parties for a speedy and peaceful settlement of the conflict. Mrs. Indira Gandhi was convinced of the wisdom of her father's remark when he said that "the fate of the world depends more on the USA, the United Kingdom, the Soviet Union, and China than on the rest of the world put together."[14]

In a statement in Washington, D.C., on March 29, 1966, Mrs. Indira Gandhi, elaborated upon India's stand on the Vietnam conflict in the following manner:

We are, like others, deeply concerned about the future of Vietnam, a near Asian neighbour. We share the world's regret that a peaceful solution has eluded that troubled land thus far despite many and varied efforts. Nevertheless, we are convinced that all of us must keep trying. The Geneva Conference could offer a way out and might yet provide the machinery for a return to the negotiating table. . . .[15]

It is well for a nation to be aware of her limitations, but it must also assume its responsibilities. Let me again refer to my opening statement, namely, "one of the primary purposes of a foreign policy is to influence the behaviour of other states." This objective was reasonably accomplished by India through her policy of non-alignment within the context of the Cold War and the bi-polarity in world politics during 1948-1962. All this had now changed. With the breaking up of the Sino-Soviet monolith on the one hand, and the loosening of some of the Western-sponsored military and political alliances, new power relationships among the nations have begun to emerge. India could no longer afford the luxury of non-involvement in such a sensitive and vital area as Southeast Asia. India needs to develop certain concrete foreign policy attitudes in this area and realistically approach the new and complex environment around her.

In her first years of independence, India was less in need of influencing the behaviour of other states vis-a-vis herself and her status, particularly within South and Southeast Asia. Circumstances have changed this. The power struggle within the hemisphere has itself touched her, and in so doing requires that she should evolve a more positive attitude toward the direction she would desire others to move. In other words, India requires a more dynamic foreign policy. Her own national interest now dictates such a course. To be objective does not mean to be above or without a policy. At most, India, until recently, had no direct stake in the clash of interests of the major powers. Today she cannot afford, in her own interest, not to.

The conflict in Vietnam well illustrated these comlexities. For instance, it was no longer a matter of "national self-determination" or "re-unification," as it was simplified within the context of anti-colonialism. The clash of issues in Vietnam continues at a higher level. The three major powers, the United States, Soviet Union, and China, had all taken different positions on how to resolve the conflict. India's relative position with each required her to develop a positive policy that focused on her own interests. Her most obvious interest was to contain the conflict within its immediate boundaries. If she intended to influence the behaviour of other nations relative to this end, she needed to reassess her previous policy. Under the prevalent circumstances, India could not hope to influence the behaviour of Communist China in any positive manner. She could, or at least should have made every effort to influence the positions held in Washington and Moscow toward Vietnam, but she could exert her influence only when she had taken a fresh and realistic look at the dangers to her national security if the Vietnam conflict had been allowed to expand or had been resolved on Peking or Hanoi's terms.

The cessation of hostilities in January 1973 and the American withdrawal from Vietnam presents a number of opportunities for India to increase her leverage, not only in Vietnam, but in Indo-China generally. She can do so, however, only by re-examining the basis of her relations with these nations. No positive and mutually supportive relations are likely to develop merely on slogans of anti-colonialism or a vague sense of Asian unity and solidarity. Concrete economic and political ties need to be fostered to provide the general substance and meaning of policy. The opportunities are present; what is needed is a sense of direction and a national re-ordering of priorities.

C. INDIA AND WEST ASIA

Apart from a certain commonality of outlook between India and the West Asian nations regarding anti-colonialism, opposition to military blocs, and solidarity with Afro-Asian nations, India's relations with the region that extends from Iran to Turkey and Southern Yemen to the United Arab Republic are subject to deep historical, economic, cultural, and political influences. West Asia, as defined by India, is an uncertain geo-political concept, and within its confines there exists great diversity. It has no overriding unity, apart from a belief in a common faith, Islam. At least three prominent national traditions have existed for a millenium, and express themselves in modern-day Turkey, Iran, and the Arab States. In this discussion, I shall not attempt to cover the broad range, but will try to illustrate the vagaries of Indian policy in this region by focusing upon Indo-Arab relations on specific issues. Before we proceed to study this particular relationship it will be well to examine briefly a few general elements that form a background to the developments and may be helpful to our understanding of the problems.

Arab influence in India dates back many centuries, to A. D. 712 when a band of Arab marauders captured the area of Sind. Further Muslim penetrations of India took another three centuries when, in A. D. 998, Mahmud of Ghazni undertook a number of looting expeditions. In 1191 a new chapter in the history of India began when Mohammed Ghori, an Afghan, invaded India and founded a Muslim kingdom in Delhi. This Muslim kingdom came to be known as the Delhi Sultanate and remained in existence from 1206 until 1526. The Delhi Sultanate, in turn, was supplanted by the Moghul (Arabic word for Mongol) Empire founded by Babur. From 1526 to 1707, when the last great Moghul Emperor Aurangzeb died, not only Islam, but a Western Asian tradition, outlook, and culture, remained as dominant factors in the country's history.

By the beginning of the eighteenth century, the territorial unity forged under the Moghuls had virtually disappeared. Many regional rulers had begun to emerge and established their autonomy. The British had also arrived in Bengal and had started taking an active role in the struggle for power among the feuding rulers. Beginning with the "Battle of Plassey" in 1757, the British domination of India began in an earnest and systematic fashion. The history of British rule is beyond the scope of our discussion here, but we should note that in many parts of India the British authority directly supplanted the Muslim rule, a rule which under several dynasties lasted seven and one-half centuries.

The impact of such a long and penetrating relationship cannot be overemphasized. Suffice it to say that a large and significant portion of the population in India remains keenly interested in the

affairs of Western Asia. This domestic compulsion alone with difficult relations with Pakistan prompted Nehru to take special pains
to keep India's fences mended in Muslim Western Asia, particularly the United Arab Republic. The Indian Council for Cultural
Relations was established in 1950 with active government help to
improve relations with Western Asia. Prominent Indian Muslims,
political leaders, scholars, and others undertook extensive tours to
attain this objective. High-level diplomacy was carried on by
Maulana Azad, a native of Western Asia before joining the Indian
Nationalist Movement, an Arabic scholar, and India's Minister
of Education from 1947 until his death in 1958. Another
distinguished Muslim, Dr. Zakir Husain, India's late President,
undertook several missions to Western Asia to offset the region's
natural learnings toward Pakistan, a Muslim state. All in
all, India, has consistently invested much effort and energy to
promote herself in the Arab world for what appear to be important objectives. Her cultural, political, and economic stakes in
the region elevate Western Asia to a position of major importance
for India's total foreign policy. In the following pages I shall
briefly review India's political and moral support for the Arab
world and evaluate whatever returns she has received on her
investment.

Generally speaking, India's support of the Arab world, and
the United Arab Republic in particular, can be grouped into
two broad categories : (1) Support for Arab nationalism and self-
determination without the intervention of the Western powers;
and (2) Support for the Arab position in the Arab-Israeli dispute.
Within the context of these broad categories, I shall attempt to
describe the relationship of issues such as opposition to the Baghdad
Pact—now called the Central Treaty Organization (CENTO),
support for Egypt's nationalization of the Suez Canal, non-criticism
of Soviet arms shipments into the area, concern for the rights of
the Palestine refugees, and other development in the region that
have implications for the world community at large.

In a speech in Lok Sabha on August 14, 1958, Nehru remarked
that India's foreign policy was "friendly to all countries, but inevitably our sympathies are with the Arab countries and with
Arab nationalism....."[16] Nehru based India's policy on the assumption that Arab nationalism was the dominant force in the
area and had to be recognized. The Western attitude of treating

the Arab countries as tender infants in need for the guardian-
ship of the bigger powers was totally unsound and did not take
into account the deep-rooted reality of Arab nationalism. Nehru
also felt that the Western theory of a "power vacuum" in West
Asia that must necessarily be filled by the Soviet Union or some
other great power, should the Western influence wane, was unwarranted and contributed to tensions in the area. India's approach to the problems of West Asia can perhaps be best illustrated
through the following statcment by Nehru:

> We are convinced that any effective solution of the problems of
> West Asia must be based on the recognition of the dominant
> urge and force of Arab nationalism. Any settlement must have
> the good will and cooperation of the Arab nations. The need
> of the European countries for oil is patent, but there should be
> no difficulty in arriving at a friendly arrangement which ensures
> the supply of oil. However, the presence of foreign forces of any
> kind in this area [a reference to American troops in Lebanon and British
> soldiers in Jordon] will be a constant, irritant, leading to trouble.
> Peace in this area will come if the area is removed from the
> orbit of the cold war[17].

It was in keeping with this appraisal that India brought its full
weight to condemn the Anglo-French intervention against Egypt
in 1956. Nehru considered the Anglo-French military operations
a flagrant case of aggression to enforce their will against Egypt,
even to the extent of changing the government of that country.
By this action India, for the first time since her independence in
1947, openly broke with her senior Commonwealth partner, the
United Kingdom, and asserted an independent position. This
fact takes on additional significance when we realize that India
at that time was overwhelmingly dependent upon the United
Kingdom for her own security requirements in terms for armament
for her defence forces.

For all practical purposes, for reasons alluded to earlier in this
chapter, India has consistently followed a pro-Arab policy in the
power politics of the area. So too with the Arab-Israeli conflict.
At the time of the creation of Israel in 1948, India had supported
the Arab position on Palestine and voted against the partition
of Palestine into "Arab and Jewish Zones of Administration"—a

euphemism for the establishment of two indepdendnt states, one Arab and other Jewish. As is well known, the 1948 hostilities between the state of Israel and the neighbouring Arab states and the subsequent armistice considerably altered the original boundaries drawn by the United Nations for the proposed two states. The post-armistice Israel became larger than was proposed earlier while the Arab zone was completely absorbed by Jordan and Egypt. The Arabs displaced from their homeland came to the abjoining states of Jordan and Egypt and to this day continue to lead a miserable existence in various refugee camps.

Despite her sympathies for the Arab cause and a feeling that grave injustice had been done to the Arabs of Palestine, India could not ignore the fact of Israel. In 1954, six years after the war, India finally recognized the state of Israel but to this day has declined to exchange diplomatic representatives. This absence of diplomats has been designed largely to avoid the displeasure of Arab states, many of whom still remain dedicated to the destruction of Israel. Other factors influencing India's stance in this situation are New Delhi's view that Israel has not been responsive to the plight of the Palestinian refugees and has generally acted in concert with the Western colonial powers against the interests of peace in the region. The premeditated Israeli action in the Sinai peninsula of Egypt in 1956 has been pointed out as an illustration of Israeli collusion with the former colonial powers of the region. Nehru, in answer to a question at a press conference on August 7, 1958, conceded that India's decision to not exchange diplomatic representatives with Israel was "not a matter of high principle," but was based on practical considerations arising out of the problems between Israel and the Arab countries.[18]

An evaluation of India's policy in West Asia clearly indicates that her pro-Arabism gravely reduced her leverage with the Western powers, especially the United Kingdom, after the 1956 Suez incident. Even Pakistan, a Muslim nation, did not go as far as India did in her censure of the Anglo-French intervention. One can trace a marked departure in British attitude toward the Kashmir dispute between India and Pakistan to the event. It is after 1956 that the British delegates in the United Nations began to support Pakistan's contentions regarding Kashmir and did not maintain their previously neutral stance among the two Commonwealth members. The message, therefore, was made abundantly clear: If India was to depart from the rules of the game in one instance, she should not expect others to abide by them.

As in 1956, 1967, and again in the 1973 Arab-Israeli hostilities, India clearly sided with the Arab countries. Both in 1956 and 1967 the Arabs lost their wars with Israel and thus caused their supporters considerable embarrassment. The situation in 1973, however, appears to be somewhat different though no clear picture has emerged as yet. Something new, however, has developed. Public opinion in India is now divided and the government's pro-Arab stand has come under heavy criticism in mass media and other forums. In 1967, the then Foreign Minister, M. C. Chagla, a Muslim, was singled out as a special object of criticism among the opposition in Parliament. He was accused of being more pro-Arab than Arabs themselves, and he subsequently resigned from his post, though officially his resignation was described as unconnected to the criticism of his handling of the situation.

What has brought about this radical departure in public mood in India regarding the Arab world? During the seventeen-year period between 1956, and 1973, three critical tests of India's pro-Arab policies came in 1962, 1965 and 1971. As these developments are discussed in greater detail in the following chapter dealing with India and her neighbours, at this point I shall refer only to the pertinent aspects bearing upon India's policy in the Arab world. In 1962, when the India-China border conflct broke out, only the governments of Lebanon, Jordan and Saudi Arabia expressed sympathy and support for India. With the exception of Saudi Arabia, the principals in the Arab world, Syria, Iraq, and the United Arab Republic, all proposed some form of mediation or arbitration of the India-China border dispute and stayed away from taking a pro-Indian position. The United Arab Republic subsequently offered a plan for mediation that appeared to be favourable to India.[19] The U.A.R. plan also called for the withdrawal of military forces behind the disputed boundary lines before negotiation.

In practical terms, these responses did not provide any satisfactory returns on the heavy political investments made by India in the area. Mediation offers are necessarily uncommitted responses and cannot be equated with India's full-fledged pro-Arab reaction in the Suez crisis of 1956. Nehru had failed to recognize

the extent of China's influence in the area and was disheartened
to learn that India must now compete with China as well as
Pakistan in the Arab world. Furthermore, as Agwani has pointed
out, Arabs are traditionally a parochial people and are generally
disinterested in the world beyond their borders.[20]

The second critical test for India's West Asia Policy came
during the Indo-Pakistan border war of 1965. Unlike the India-
China conflict, the Indo-Pakistan border war brought into focus
India's efforts at offsetting the Islamic factor among the Arab
states and Pakistan. The earlier Turkish and Iranian alignment
with Pakistan had already considerably "damaged India's
efforts to keep the Islamic factor from reinforcing Pakistan in
geo-political and ideological terms."[21] There is some validity in
President Ayub Khan's remark that Pakistan's entry into the
Baghdad Pact (CENTO) was motivated by the opportunity for
developing the organization into a potential forum for the
Muslim countries and to deflect India's policy in West Asia.[22]
Nevertheless, India had hoped that sympathy, understanding,
and support from the Arab states regarding her quarrels with
Pakistan would be based upon the merits of the issues; and she
especially had hoped to keep the religious consideration between
Pakistan and the Arab states out of the picture. As is well known,
India was sorely disappointed in her expectations.

At the very outbreak of the Indo-Pakistan hostilities, Jordan
fully backed the Pakistani position in the United Nations debates.
Soon after, along with Saudi Arabia, she demanded a collective
Arab condemnation of India's stand on the issue at the Casa-
blanca Conference of the Arab heads of states. The passage
of this resolution was blocked mainly by President Nasser,
an event that was more an indication of the prestige Nasser
enjoyed in the Arab world rather than a success story of Indian
diplomacy. The final communique issued at the conference on
September 17, 1965, did not support the Indian position, called
for cessation of hostilities, and urged India and Pakistan to arrive
at a negotiated settlement of their dispute in accordance with the
principles and resolutions of the United Nations.[23]

Thus for the second time within three years, India's West Asian
political investment paid only marginal dividends. In reality, it
was the United Arab Republic that through its influence and
prestige procured a neutral Arab stance in 1962 and averted open

condemnation of India in 1965. To the extent that India's close relations with the United Arab Republic were concerned, Indian policy may be assigned a passing grade. But in the larger context of developments, Indians had begun to question the high cost of the U.A.R.'s neutrality. Consequently, when the Government of India, once again, openly sided with the Arabs in the Arab-Israeli conflict of 1967, the popular uproar was an indication of the public's keen awareness of how the Arab states let India down in her hour of need.

As was the case in 1965, the Arab nations supported Pakistan during the Indo-Pakistan war again in 1971, even though this time the cause for the hostilities was directly related to Pakistani leaders own policies of denial of self-rule and brutal suppression of a majority of its people living in the eastern wing. The pro-Pakistan stand of the Arab nations, consequently, appeared totally irrational to the people of India and has further crystalized their distrust of the Arab Leaders.

The conclusion is inescapeable: the mere fact of the historic, cultural, and religious ties between India and West Asia is simply not a sufficient basis for any sustained and mutually supportive relationship. India needs to define her interests in the area specifically and selectively. In other words, India needs to choose her friends in the region on the basis of common interests and expectations for the future. The continued exclusion of Israel in India's policy in West Asia is not only patently absurd but potentially harmful for India's interests, far beyond the confines of the Arab world.

NOTES

[1] For a brief discussion of this point see T. Walter Wallbank, *A Short History of India and Pakistan* (New York: The New American Library, Mentor Books, 1958), pp. 35-53. For a general historical survey see K.M. Panikkar, *A Survey of Indian History* (Bombay: Asia Publishing House, 1956).

[2] Inaugural speech at the Asian Relations Conference, New Delhi, March 23, 1947. Reproduced in *Jawaharlal Nehru's Speeches*, Vol. I, (1946-1959), (Delhi: Publications Division, Government of India, 1949), p. 303.

[3] Address before the Conference of Heads of State of Governments of Non-aligned Countries, Beograd, September 1, 1961 (Washington, D. C.: Embassy of Indonesia) (Mimeo) pp. 6-7.

[4] Bimla Prasad, *The Origins of Indian Foreign Policy* (Calcutta: Bookland, 1962);

and K. S. Murty, *Indian Foreign Policy*, 1964.

[5] *Panchsheel* or five principles of peaceful coexistence. These are: (*i*) Mutual respect for each other's territorial integrity and sovereignty; (*ii*) Non-aggression; (*iii*) Non-interference in each other's internal affairs; (*iv*) Equality and mutual benefit; and (*v*) Peaceful coexistence.

[6] "Prime Minister Nehru's 6-Point Plan for Indo-China," in S. L. Poplai (ed.), *The Temper of Peace* (New Delhi: Indian Council of World Affairs, 1955), pp. 3-4.

[7] "The Joint Statement by Mr. Nehru and Mr. Ho Chi Minh," in *Foreign Policy of India—Texts of Decuments* (New Delhi : Lok Sabha Secretariat, 1958; p. 115.

[8] *Foreign Policy of India, op. cit.*, pp. 153-154.

[9] Articles 6 & 7 of the final declaration of the Geneva Agreements.

[10] For a detailed discussion of this point, see Ton That Thien, *India and Southeast Asia—1947-1960* (Geneva: Librairie Droz, 1963), pp. 119-149.

[11] International Commission for Supervision and Control in Vietnam : *Interim Reports* (Twelve Reports from 1954-62).

[12] ICSC, Vietnam, *Tenth Report*, Cmnd. 1040 (1960), pp. 13 and 26.

[13] Ton That Thien, *op. cit.*, p. 148.

[14] *Jawaharlal Nehru's Speeches*, 1949-53 (New Delhi : The Publications Division, 1954), p. 178.

[15] *Extracts of Statements Explaining India's Views on Vietnam* (Washington, D. C. : Information Ser vices of India) (Mimeo), pp. 1-10.

[16] Jawaharlal Nehru, *India's Foreign Policy* (New Delhi : Publications Division, Government of India, 1961), p. 281.

[17] *Ibid.*, p. 283.

[18] *Ibid.*, pp. 414-415.

[19] For a detailed discussion, see M. S. Agwani, "The Reaction of West Asia and the U. A. R." [to the Sino-Indian conflict of 1962], *International Studies*, Vol. V (July-October, 1963), pp. 75-79.

[20] *Ibid.*, p. 75.

[21] Paul F. Power, "India and West Asia," Paper presented at the 17th Annual Meeting of the Midwest Conference on Asian Affairs, October 31—November 2, 1967, Western Michigan University, Kalamazoo, Michigan (Mimeo), p. 7.

[22] Ayub Khan, *op. cit.*, p. 155.

[23] For the text of the communique see *UAR News*, September, 1955.

CHAPTER V

INDIA AND HER NEIGHBOURS

IN THIS CHAPTER I shall conclude our discussion of India's foreign policy by analyzing her relations with some selected nations falling within our third theoretical concentric circle. As indicated earlier, this closest-to-home circle received proportionately less attention and nations within it were shown only a meagre concern by India's policy-makers. This is not to say that India was free of problems in her relations with these neighbouring countries. Quite the contrary. Nevertheless, in view of the vital importance of these neighbours to her national interests, not enough energy, imagination, or cooperation and accommodation were exhibited by India's leaders beginning with Nehru, then Shastri and now, to a large extent, Mrs. Gandhi.

Pakistan, Afghanistan, Nepal, China, Burma, Ceylon, and the new nation of Bangladesh (formerly East Pakistan), are India's closest neighbours and share many common historical, cultural, social, economic, and political bonds with her. These neighbours possess a varied and complex set of foreign policy orientations, and their individual attitudes towards India differ accordingly. Of the seven nations mentioned above, Pakistan and China remain the two crucial elements in the formulation and development of India's foreign policy. The decision-makers in India cannot ignore the *realpolitik* of the situation as it prevails in the region. Strange though it may seem, despite the encouraging developments during the years 1972 and 1973, Pakistan continues to remain an important concern of Indian planners and is considered a greater de-stabilizing factor in the subcontinent than even China. This assessment is based on the belief that an India-China conflict cannot remain localized and must, in due course, involve other nations to restore the power imbalance and strengthen the Indian side.

A conflict with Pakistan, on the other hand, may not evoke a similar response in world capitals who may regard it as only a "local" matter." Pakistan, despite her flirtation with China, is

still considered an ally of the West. It enjoys considerable support
both in the United States and the United Kingdom. Moreover,
the potential source of any major Indo-Pakistan conflict is likely
to be the ultimate status of the state of Kashmir. Although New
Delhi regards Kashmir's accession to India as final and the dispute as closed, her position has not been fully accepted by Pakistan and many of Pakistan's friends and allies. India's strategy,
therefore, is fashioned to cope with potential renewed conflicts
with her neighbours to the north and is based on the above mentioned analysis of the situation on her borders.

In excluding a discussion of India's relations with other neighbours, I do not wish to minimize either the importance of outstanding issues between them or their significance in the South
Asian political arena. Afghanistan's role in Indo-Pakistan relations,
the Nepal and Sino-Indian political chess game, the question of
the people of Indian origin in Ceylon and its impact on Indo-
Ceylonese relations, the emerging delicate relations with Bangladesh, etc., all are important issues in the total range of problems
and opportunities in the region. But, for the analysis of Indian
foreign policy undertaken in this study, a discussion of these
issues would have marginal value and would not alter my central
argument. I have, therefore, confined my discussion in this
chapter to India's relations with Pakistan and China.

A. INDIA AND PAKISTAN

Historically, geographically, linguistically, culturally, and economically, perhaps no other two countries in the world have so
much in common as India and Pakistan. What became two nations in 1947 developed for ages as integral parts of a single economic and political entity. As Sisir Gupta has pointed out:

> The political leaders who conceived Pakistan and the leaders
> of India's struggle for freedom were close associates and collea-
> gues, believing in a common set of values. Economically, the
> two countries have been traditionally interdependent. . . . The
> cotton textile mills in Bombay would assure a minimum price to
> the cotton growers of West Punjab. . . . The same literary figures
> are held in esteem by Indians and Pakistanis . . . . Members of the
> same family often reside in both countries. . .[1].

It is, therefore, especially unfortunate that India and Pakistan have had difficulty while living with each other in peace and harmony. In deference to their past close ties, a desire for peaceful mutual relations continues to be expressed in official statements of policy.

From the beginning, many issues contributed to the persistent hostile relation between India and Pakistan, among them the recovery of abducted persons, protection of shrines and holy places, exchange of movable evacuee property, sharing of canal waters from Indian headworks, and the status of Kashmir. With the exception of Kashmir, workable, though unspectacular, agreements were negotiated in other spheres. The Kashmir issue, on the other hand, with the exception of the war over Bangladesh issue in 1971, has had a continuously adverse effect on Indo-Pakistan relations since these two countries became independent nations over a quarter century ago. During this long period, the strategies of both the principals, India and Pakistan, and other interested nations, the United States, the Soviet Union, and China, have shifted from time to time;[2] but the basic goal of their foreign policies, i.e. to influence the behaviour of others in their favour, has not changed. From their initial support of one nation or the other, both the United States and the Soviet Union now appear to have similar objectives: to promote an amicable and peaceful settlement of the existing conflicts so that the two countries may better utilize their own limited resources, as well as foreign assistance, toward economic development and the maintenance of national security and independence. The long-term objectives of China's partisan policy of supporting Pakistan on almost every issue are not yet clear. Her immediate goal, however, appears to be a desire to influence developments in South Asia, an area previously free of her influence.

Despite a series of lengthy, tiring, and patient attempts by many individuals, nations, and organizations, a solution to the Kashmir issue acceptable to both India and Pakistan has yet to emerge. This failure continues, largely because the intermediaries directed their efforts mainly at the obvious and stated historical, legal, and political merits of the case. The real and basic factors responsible for conflict and tension between India and Pakistan, however, have been implicit and unstated. Most important of these were (1) Pakistan's desire to be treated as India's co-equal in political and military terms, and (2) Pakistan's notion that she was somehow the sole spokesman of the Muslims in the subcontinent including Kashmir. Needless to say, India's decision-makers were not disposed to accept these assumptions for a variety of sound reasons. Let me now briefly elaborate on these two points in the context of Indo-Pakistan relations generally and the Kashmir issue in particular.

1. Pakistan's Drive for Political Equality with India

It is unfortunate that Pakistan's foreign policy has tended to begin and end at her borders. It mattered little whether she joined a military alliance, such as CENTO and SEATO*, against a possible threat from international Communism or attempted to form a Pan-Islamic Union of Muslim states, as she did from 1947 to 1952, joined in a mutual assistance pact with the United States, or cultivated a specially close relationship with China as she did in the aftermath of India-China border conflict of 1962; the be-all and end-all of Pakistan's foreign policy has been an implacable distrust and dislike of India and India's status in the international community. As Bhabani Sen Gupta pointed out: "The Indian Image of Pakistan and the Pakistani image of India are etched out of the historical past of the Muslim conquest and rule of Hindustan rather than the recent memories of British domination of an undivided India."[3]

While some sections of political opinion in India may indeed distrust Pakistan's motives, it must be said to the credit of India's leaders that they have repeatedly and consistently tried to foster mutually beneficial and friendly relations with Pakistan. In a speech at the Indian Council of World Affairs in March, 1949, Nehru remarked :

In regard to Pakistan the position has been a very peculiar one owing to the way Pakistan was formed and India was divided. And there have not only been all the upsets that you know but something much deeper, and that is a complete emotional upset of all the people in India and Pakistan because of this. It is a very difficult thing to deal with, a psychological thing, which cannot be dealt with superficially.... There is no doubt at all in my mind that it is inevitable for India and Pakistan to have

* Pakistan officially withdrew from SEATO in November 1973.

close relations, very close relations, some time or other in the future I cannot state when this will take place, but situated as we are, with all our past we cannot be just indifferent neighbours We can be either rather hostile to each other or very friendly with each other. Ultimately we can only be really very friendly, whatever period of hostility may intervene in between because our interests are so closely interlinked[4]

Nehru's optimism was obviously based on a rational analysis of the conditions in the Indo-Pakistan sub continent. The irony of Indo-Pakistan relations, however, has been the irrational attitude of Pakistan, and this fact has continued to frustrate the growth of normal and friendly relations between the two countries Although friendly relations have eluded the two neighbours for over a quarter of a century, the essence of India's policy toward Pakistan has been an attempt to live in peace with her India sought to reassure Pakistan of her peaceful intentions by offering to sign a "no-war declaration" in February, 1950. Pakistan rejected this offer and indicated that such an offer was meaningless unless other outstanding disputes—meaning Kashmir—had first been resolved. In terms of such a response one is tempted to ask: What might be the point of a no-war declaration if no disputes existed between any two countries? In other words, Pakistan's negative response to India's offer was an implicit acknowledgement that she did not rule out the use of force to settle her outstanding disputes with India

During the 1947-1951 period, India mainly followed a *status quo* policy toward Pakistan, a policy aimed at keeping the tensions between the two countries low without surrendering anything at all on any vital issue. This Indian policy of fighting with a smile and always being prepared for a friendly handshake apparently irked Pakistan, who viewed this posture as a patronizing attempt to maintain a regionally dominant position. The depth of emotions in "Muslim Pakistan" against a "Hindu India"[5] rendered all Indian attempts at reconciliation, however genuine, fruitless

In the early years of tension and conflict, Pakistan sought to influence India through pressure from other powerful capitals, mainly London and Washington, where she enjoyed a great fund of goodwill. The British sympathies for Pakistan were natural and understandable; after all, the partition of India was as much their

brain-child as of M. A. Jinnah and the Muslim League. Furthermore, it was the Indian Nationalist Movement that started the
break-up of the British Empire. By contrast, the American support
for Pakistani claims against India is indeed intriguing. As is now
well known, this development did not come about due to Pakistan's
efforts but was engineered by the British Government. Until recently, the United States Government tended to follow British advice
regarding events in South Asia, supposedly on the grounds of
British expertise in the area. Needless to say, the consequences of
such a course of action have been full of pitfalls and have caused
grave resentments against United States policies in many countries
in the region, particularly in India.

A critic has stated that a major "cause of Indian hostility is
that, according to India, the sole objective of Pakistan's foreign
policy is to undermine the influence of India and demonstrate to
the world that Pakistan is in no way a smaller power than India"⁶
I do not propose to argue with the essential content of the statement inasmuch as it deals with Pakistan's attempts to try to be
India's military and political equal. As stated earlier, the deep
historical and psychological dimensions of Hindu-Muslim relations
have continued to prevent Pakistan from taking a realistic look at
her position toward India After all, Pakistan is less than a quarter
of India's size and contains about one-eighths of India's human
resources, and cannot alter the power balance in South Asia even
by borrowing strength from abroad

The contention that Indo-Pakistan tensions and conflicts are due
to India's hostility toward her neighbour are simply not borne
out by the facts. It was Pakistan, not India, who sought military
allies wherever she could find them. Pakistan's entry into the
West-sponsored SEATO and CENTO military alliances had
nothing to do with fighting the international communist danger
and was patently designed to improve her bargaining power with
India When the intended results were not forthcoming, Pakistan,
in an abrupt about-face, started courting the very same nations,
the Soviet Union and China, against whom she had ostensibly
joined these military pacts. Pakistan's foreign policy and diplomacy during the entire period of 1954-1970 bears testimony to
this conclusion. Let me support this point by presenting an evaluation of India's attitude toward Pakistan by an Australian diplomat with wide knowledge of the subject :

On the issues dividing India and Pakistan, with one exception only, Nehru always insisted, often against the advice or wishes of his ministers or his senior officials, on the generous view and on giving Pakistan the benefit of the doubt. This was so in the case of financial disputes, in the canal waters affair, in frontier readjustments and in movements of persons. . . . The one exception was Kashmir . . . ."[7]

This one exception, Kashmir, will be discussed below within the context of Pakistan's second assumption of being the spokesman for the Muslims in the subcontinent.

2. Pakistan—A Spokesman for Muslims in the Subcontinent?

Communal strife has had a long and ugly history in the subcontinent. In 1947 it was mainly responsible for the partition of India and Pakistan. The creation of Pakistan as a separate Muslim homeland, however, was not emulated in India, who set out to build a secular, democratic republic. Nehru considered the mixture of religion and politics a dangerous alliance that would result in terrible consequsences.[8]

The goal of a secular India is yet to be fully achieved. Communal harmony has been disturbed too often for India's conform, but, despite setbacks, secularism and national unity in India have been growing. Education, industrialization, urbanization, and the growing political sophistication of the nation are beginning to neutralize the religious drag on the forward movement of the idea. In short, I may say that the sustained and persistent endeavours of India's leaders during the formative stages of nation-building have finally begun to pay some dividends, and the Indian people have laid the foundation of a new kind of political life.

Pakistan's constant propaganda, suggesting that despite all its secularism India is no more than a Hindu state and that Muslims in India were treated as second-class citizens, stemmed from its stand as the spokesman of Muslims in the subcontinent. The often repeated fact that the Indian National Congress did not accept the partition of India because it accepted the theory of two nations, one Muslim and the other Hindu, but only as a pragmatic solution to obtain British withdrawal from the country seemed purposely lost on Pakistani leaders. Partly, this propaganda may well have been due to the enormous problems of stabilizing a structurally unique, if not absurd, state. Instead of pursuing a set of concrete and constructive policies to promote a positive Pakistani identity, the Pakistani leaders chose a less demanding method of keeping the country together ; and the religious issues appeared to be the most convenient one to employ against India. Consequently, a whole range of normal and usual problems between the two countries were given a communal stance. The Kashmir issue must be viewed in this context.

The "supremely beautiful woman,"[9] Kashmir shares a common border with four nations—Pakistan, Afghanistan, China and the U. S. S. R.—and occupies a strategic position for India. Kashmir has an area of 86,000 square miles and a population of about 4 million. Much of the state is hills and snow-covered peaks. The most important region in the state is the Vale of Kashmir, which is eighty-five miles long and twenty-five miles wide and contains over sixty per cent of the states' population. Despite the homogeneity, one might infer from the heavy predominance of Muslims, Kashmir is a nation divided by its mountains, its gods, its traditions, its allegiances, and the temperament of its people. It is important to note that Kashmir has five distinct regions— Jammu, The Valley, Ladakh, the Hill Districts, and the Tribal Areas. Under the present *de facto* partition of the state, except for the Hill Districts, no other sub-groups in Kashmir are divided. Jammu, The Valley, and Ladakh are in India ; the Tribal Areas are in Pakistan (or Azad [Free] Kashmir); and only the Hill Districts (mainly Poonch) are divided among India and Pakistan.

The legal and political history of the Kashmir issue is well known, and I need not go into details here. The essentials of the dispute, however, are crucial to an understanding of the problem and are worth recapitulating.

With the announcement of a date for the transfer of power from tht British Government to India and Pakistan, the native Indian states were informed that His Majesty's Government would cease to exercise the powers of paramountcy over them. This meant that the rights of the states which flowed from their relationship to the British Crown no longer existed and all the rights that were surrendered by the states to the paramount power returned to the states. Though in theory the native states could thus declare themselves independent, they were strongly advised to accede to

India or Pakistan in accordance with social, geographical, and other considerations. Given Kashmir's geographic location and physical size, the Maharaja contemplated independence and postponed the question of accession to either India or Pakistan. Three days before the transfer of power (August 12, 1947), the Maharaja proposed a "standstill agreement" to India and Pakistan. The agreement sought the continuance of normal communication services and economic understanding while the ruler took more time to make up his mind.

Pakistan agreed and as a result continued to operate the postal and telegraphic services in Kashmir. India at the time remained uncommitted. But within a month of the "standstill agreement," Pakistan started to harass the state's population by stopping economic activities and food and fuel supplies. The economic boycott appeared to be designed to force Kashmir's accession to Pakistan. The Maharaja, however, did not show any disposition to accede, and his reluctance brought military pressure from Pakistan.

Beginning in early October, 1947, the Afridi and Mahsud tribesmen of the North-West Frontier (thus a responsibility of Pakistan) invaded Kashmir. On October 15, nearly 5,000 raiders began the siege of Fort Owen inside Kashmir, and by October 22, infiltrations and raids were transformed into a full-scale military attack upon the state of Kashmir. Although it appeared that Kashmir was in imminent danger of falling to the invaders, Lord Mountbatten, India's Governor-General, advised Nehru not to send any aid without the formal accession of Kashmir to India. On October 24, the legally constituted Government of Kashmir, of which the Maharaja was the head and with whom Pakistan had earlier entered into the "standstill agreement," acceded the state to India and requested urgent military help against the invaders. India accepted the Instrument of Accession signed by the Maharaja and supported by the Kashmir National Conference (the popular political party) and immediately flew troops into the state. India, in its acceptance of the Instrument of Accession, however, pledged that "as soon as law and order have been restored in Kashmir and her soil cleared of the invaders" the question of the states' accession should be ratified by the people as well.

It is important to remember that India was not required to make such a pledge to anyone. Moreover, up to this point, Pakistan had never suggested that the future of Kashmir should be determined by the wishes of the people. Pakistan was apparently confident of a military conquest of Kashmir through the proxy invasion, so that the arrival of the Indian army in Kashmir on October 27 upset the Pakistani time-table for victory. Still hoping for a military solution, according to Campbell-Johnson, Aide to Lord Mountbatten, M. A. Jinnah, Governor-General of Pakistan, ordered Pakistani troops to enter Kashmir on October 27, 1947. However, when the British Commander-in-Chief of the Pakistani Army, General Auchinleck, pointed out that an act of direct invasion would involve withdrawal of British officers serving with the Pakistani Army, Jinnah cancelled the orders the following day.[10]

Even though Pakistan officially did not enter Kashmir, the scale and extent of her unofficial participation in the invasion came to light soon after the Indian Army engaged the invaders in battle. The Government of India repeatedly asked the Government of Pakistan to desist from such activities, but Pakistan never bothered to respond. Finally, on December 31, 1947, Nehru informed the Prime Minister of Pakistan, Liaqat Ali Khan, that India had decided to refer the Kashmir question to the Security Council of the United Nations and to request the Council to ask the Government of Pakistan :

(i) to prevent Pakistan Government personnel, military and civil, participating in or assisting the invasion of Jammu and Kashmir State ;

(ii) to call upon other Pakistan nationals to desist from taking any part in the fighting in Jammu and Kashmir State ;

(iii) to deny to the invaders :

(a) access to and use of its territory for operations against Kashmir ;

(b) military and other supplies ;

(c) all other kinds of aid that might tend to prolong the present struggle.[11]

The central issue, according to India, was Pakistan's complicity in the invasion of Kashmir. The U. N. Security Council, however, emphasized the question of self-determination by the people o f Kashmir and thus questioned the state's accession to India, which, it said, gave Pakistan a *locus standi* in the case. India agreed to carry out her promises to the people of Kashmir, provided that Pakistan withdrew its armed forces, tribesmen, and other nationals from Kashmir. The Security Council's resolution of Jaunary 5, 1949, proposed a plebiscite under the auspices of the Government of Jammu and Kashmir ; affirmed the right of the Indian Army to defend the state ; and called for the withdrawal of Pakistani forces and other elements.[12]

Pakistan continuously refused to withdraw her forces from Kashmir, and thus, according to India, made the resolution inoperative and ineffective. In realistic terms, the Kashmir issue was never simply a legal issue that could have been decided in the United Nations. Josef Korbel has aptly described it as an "uncompromising and perhaps uncompromisable struggle of two ways of life, two concepts of political organization, two scales of values, two spiritual attitudes, that find themselves locked in deadly conflict, a conflict in which Kashmir has become both symbol and battleground."[13]

In reality, a resolution of the Kashmir dispute, essential in Pakistan's view for peace with India, could never be based on the Hindu-Muslim two-nation theory. Whatever chance there might have been for some other *modus vivendi* to ease tensions between the two countries further receded with the announcement of American military assistance to Pakistan in 1954 and Pakistan's subsequent entry into West-sponsored military alliances. Any United Nations action regarding Kashmir, unacceptable to India, was virtually ruled out due to Soviet support of India's stand on the issue.

Pakistan had hoped that her entry into the West-sponsored alliances would pay some political dividends in increasing her military strength in relation to India's, and win the American and British diplomatic support for her demands in Kashmir. It is common knowledge that both the United States and the United Kingdom exerted pressure on India to accommodate Pakistan's demands in Kashmir, but, as indicated earlier, both of these friends really never fully understood the depth of symbolism surrounding Kashmir. Their pressure continued regularly, but to no avail. The most intense pressure, however, was exerted immediately after the India-China conflict of 1962 and was again resisted by India.

The India-China conflict created an entirely new situation in South Asia. Not only did it jar the Indian leaders out of their complacency for having been humiliated by their former friends, but it put even the nation's security into jeopardy. In order to meet this new challenge, India abandoned her previous reservations about receiving military assistance. The United States was prompt in her response to India's requests, and later on the Soviet Union responded favourably. Pakistan, who for so long had sought to build an image of being the only reliable ally of the West in South Asia, felt her bargaining power eroding rapidly.

With the military build-up of India in response to the Chinese threat, Pakistani leaders felt that a military solution to the Kashmir issue was passing them by. Pakistan further concluded that her formal allies, the United States and the United Kingdom, were no longer useful in her ambitions in Kashmir. Following the old dictum—my enemy's enemy is my friend—Pakistan started her overtures toward China for military and political support against India. Confident of military pressure from China against India, and hoping to keep India off balance on two fronts, Pakistan first tested India's determination to fight in April, 1965, in the Rann of Kutch. India's Prime Minister Lal Bahadur Shastri's conciliatory response was obviously misread by Pakistani President Ayub Khan. Shastri's acceptance of arbitration of the dispute was viewed as a sign of Indian weakness and an emboldened Pakistan undertook a military adventure in Kashmir.

TABLE V-I

PAKISTAN GOVERNMENT'S ESTIMATES OF LOSSES IN MEN
AND MATERIAL

Item	Pakistan	India
Men killed	1,033	9,500
Tanks lost	165	475
Aircraft destroyed	14	110

SOURCE : Statement of the Defence Ministry of Pakistan,
December 4, 1965.

TABLE V-II

INDIAN GOVERNMENT'S ESTIMATES OF LOSSES IN MEN
AND MATERIAL

Item	Pakistan	India
Men killed	4,802	1,333
Tanks lost	475	128
Aircraft destroyed	73	35

SOURCE : Statement of the Defence Ministry of India,
September 25, 1965.

The three-week Indo-Pakistan War in September 1965, for all
practical purposes, was Pakistan's last attempt to annex Kashmir
by force. This undeclared, though very real war, was expensive
to both the countries. Tables V-I and V-IIi llustrate the intensity
of the conflict.

Even when some generous allowances are made for under-
statements and exaggerations, the loss of life and material for a
three-week war is substantial. The obvious question arises : Is
Kashmir worth it ? As far as India is concerned, the answer is
yes. Kashmir to India is not merely a piece of real estate or four
million people. It is symbolic of Indian secularism. If Kashmir
was to be acceded to Pakistan simply because the majority of her
population was Muslim, the entire fabric of Indian national unity
will be severely endangered. No government in India can afford
to allow such a development.

The soundness of the Indian argument was further strengthened
during the 1970-71 developments in Pakistan. Despite the element
of a common religious faith, the people of East Pakistan did not
wish to remain a part of Pakistan. The landslide victory of Shiekh
Mujeebur Rehman's-Awami League in the 1970 elections clearly
demonstrated that a mere slogan of Muslim unity was nothing
but a spent force in this second half of the twentieth century ; if
it wished to survive in the 1970's, Pakistan had to move toward
progressive economic and social policies of its own ; anti-Indian
slogans were not enough and had lost their appeal.

What began as a demand for autonomy for East Pakistan,

soon became the struggle for an independent Bangladesh in response
to the heavy and brutal military measures of West Pakistan.
It should have been, however, very clear to Pakistani rulers from
the outset that neither East Bengal nor the government and people
of India could forever tolerate the inhuman subjugation of 75
million people. The following Indo-Pakistan war during December 1971, however lamentable, became the only available solution
to an intolerable situation. *India did not dismember Pakistan. Pakistan
committed suicide.*

In the light of Pakistan's denial of self-determination to its
own people in the former East Pakistan, its claims now can
hardly be given credence in Kashmir, even on a philosophical
basis. The Pakistan of the 'seventies represents little beyond
being a political and geographic entity comprised of West Punjab,
Northwest Frontier Province, Sind, and Baluchistan. The sooner
its leaders acknowledge this reality, the sooner they can lay the
foundations of a peaceful and cooperative relationship with India
and Bangladesh and South Asia generally.

B. INDIA AND CHINA

India and China have five thousand years of national existence
behind them. During this long span of their histories, both have
been victors and vanquished many a time. But despite their
ancient contacts, which some scholars date as far back as 221
B.C.,[14] India and China never engaged in war against each other
until 1962. Still, Sino-Indian relations have not been continuous.
Perhaps the most active contacts between the two countries
prevailed during the introduction of Buddhism into China from
India beginning in the year 2 B.C., thereafter, large numbers of
monks, students, and scholars travelled across the national
borders. In a speech at a banquet held in honour of Premier Chou
En-lai of China in New Delhi on June 26, 1954, Nehru under-
lined this historical relationship in the following manner:

The past two thousand years stand witness to our mutual
relations. We have been neighbours during this stretch of years
and we have been vital countries throwing out our thoughts and
cultures to each other and to other neighbouring countries. Our
people have come into contact in many lands, more especially

in Southest Asia; yet there is no record of war between us. This long period is of peaceful commerce of ideas, of religion, and of art and culture.

Both China and India have their particular and individual backgrounds. Each has her own special cultural inheritance. In many ways they are different, and they have grown according to their own genius. Yet, in spite of these differences, we have been good neighbours and friends and have not come into conflict with each other during the millennia of history.

This is the witness of the past, and as we stand on the fine edge of the present in this turbulent world of ours, we can learn a lesson from that past, which will help us in the present and in the future....

Destiny beckons to our countries and I hope that neither of them will be found wanting at this great moment of history. I hope that our two countries will stand for peace and will live amicably together and cooperate together in the cause of peace and human advance as they have done through the past two thousand years of human history.[16]

Peace and friendly relations with China formed an important core of Nehru's foreign policy. India extended official recognition to the Peoples Republic on December 30, 1949. Despite some friction between the two countries during 1950-51, mainly arising out of the Chinese misunderstanding of India's attitude on Tibet, Nehru's patient cultivation of friendship with China began to show some results with the Korean settlement in 1953. In this context, it will be useful to recall that India did not brand China an aggressor for her entry into the Korean War in 1950 in support of the North Korean regime. This action was heavily criticized by India's Western friends, particularly the United States. Considerable Western pressure notwithstanding, Nehru pursued his policy of building a special relationship with China and toward this end championed the cause of China's entry into the United Nations beginning in September 1950.

Beginning in June 1954, with the arrival of Chou En-lai in India on a state visit and the subsequent joint statement by the Indian and Chinese Prime Ministers putting forth the doctrine of *Panch Sheela,* or the five principles of peaceful coexistence, Nehru visualized that the era of "Hindi-Chini, Bhai Bhai" (Indians and

Chinese are brothers) had finally arrived. The doctrine of *Panch Sheela* stipulated the following relations which, it was hoped, would become the basis of relations among other nations as well.

(1) Mutual respect for each other's territorial integrity and sovereignty;
(2) Mutual non-aggression;
(3) Mutual non-interference in each other's internal affairs;
(4) Equality and mutual benefit;
(5) Peaceful coexistence.

Within the framework of these principles, India signed an agreement with China in 1954, formally recognizing China's sovereignty over Tibet. Nehru played a leading role in providing China a prominent position at the Afro-Asian Conference held at Bandung in April 1955. In short, India-China relations between 1954-1957 period touched their high point and their manifestations were widespread. Beginning in 1958, India-China border problems began to emerge with some regularity and intensity. It is obvious that three to four years of friendly relations is a short period of time for any two neighbours, especially when one has expanded considerable effort and energy as India had done in this instance. Again, we can ask: Why did it happen?

The broken dialogue and conflict between India and China are not easily explained, as a complex set of circumstances prevailed throughout the 1957-62 period. Let me analyze the developments as I see them now in the light of available informations and personal interviews with many key leaders in India during my three visits in 1964, 1967 and 1970-71.

In my earlier discussion of Indo-Soviet relations, I pointed out that, beginning in 1955-1956, the Soviet leaders responded more than enthusiastically to Nehru's cultivation of a specially close relationship with the U.S.S.R. It bears repeating that this development was not necessarily prompted by the Soviet Union's desire to help India *per se*. This Soviet thrust was also designed to promote a counter-balance to the growing Chinese militancy in international affairs by shoring up India's economic and military capabilities. Furthermore, the now well-known Sino-Soviet split had reached a decisive and critical stage by 1957. As Premier Nikita S. Khrushchev's *Memoirs* indicated, in his view, a Sino-

Soviet reconciliation appeared extremely unlikely because the Chinese were so obstinate on matters dividing the two communist powers. [16] Nehru may not have been fully aware of this development, but the Chinese leaders began to be suspicious of India's close relations with the Soviets. In essence, I contend that Nehru, perhaps unknowingly, fell into the Soviet scheme of introducing a wedge between India and China. The Chinese, in turn, revived their claims upon Indian territory and started to put pressure upon her. This assumption is especially appealing when we recall that earlier in 1955 Nehru drew Premier Chou En-lai's attention to Chinese maps showing parts of Indian territory as belonging to China; Chou merely dismissed them as old Kuomintang publications that the new regime had not gotten around to revising.

What was to turn into the India-China border war in 1962 began with occasional incursions by armed Chinese military parties along the India-China border in the Northwest and Northeast regions starting in 1955. During the 1955-56 period, however, there were only four such incidents, and the situation did not seem to cause the Indian Government any serious concern. In November 1956, Chou En-lai visited India and the question of the India-China border came under review. The Chinese Premier expressed the opinion that there were no disputes regarding the border and that certain petty problems that might exist should be amicably settled by the representatives of the two governments. Chou En-lai further stated that, in regard to Burma, the Government of China had accepted and formalized the boundary drawn in 1914 (the "McMahon Line") and saw no reason why a similar arrangement could not be made with India also. Obviously, the Chinese Premier was willing to make necessary adjustments with India provided India could offer something in return. Apparently, Nehru was either oblivious to such an implication or felt that he did not have to make any concessions to China.

Beginning in October, 1957, when a Chinese party entered Walong in the Lohit Frontier Division of the North East Frontier Agency (N. E. F. A.) of India, border incursions assumed a certain pattern and frequency. During subsequent months and years, the Chinese Government advanced formal claims to some 50,000 square miles of Indian territory in N. E. F. A. and the Aksai Chin part of Ladakh. Intermittent attempts at a peacefully negotiated settlement followed throughout much of 1958-60, but to no avail.

The most serious attempt to settle the border issue was made when Chou En-lai came to Delhi in April 1960, and engaged in discussions with Nehru and Krishna Menon for six days. I have been given to understand by several knowledgeable persons in Delhi that Chou En-lai offered to formalize the India-China border in the Northeast Sector in accordance with the "McMahon Line" provided that Nehru agreed to recognize the Chinese claims to the Aksai Chin area in the Northwest, where the Chinese had already built a road and were in physical control of the territory. Given that the Chinese were in a militarily stronger position in this sector, India would have been both wise and realistic to come to a settlement with China. Nehru, however, firmly stuck to India's legal claims[17] to the area and refused to negotiate any settlement based on political or military considerations.

After the failure of this high-level attempt for a negotiated settlement, the India-China border incidents increased both in numbers and intensity. Other attempts of negotiation at lower levels were merely futile academic exercises and did not have any chance of success. The downhill trend continued rather steadily and culminated in the India-China border war of October 1962.[18] The question here is the efficacy and political wisdom of Nehru's decision not to agree to a settlement with Chou En-lai in 1960. It may well be that Nehru sincerely believed that the Chinese would adhere to the 1954 India-China declaration of *Panch Sheela*, but, as his own words at the time indicated, he was living in an artificial atmosphere of his own creation and the Chinese attack finally shook him out of it.

In my judgment, the most critical reason for the break-up of the India-China friendship was Nehru's lack of appreciation or a fuller recognition of the power axiom in the relationships between the two countries. Nehru made the cardinal blunder of neglecting India's strength while pursuing friendship with China. History shows us no illustrations where two competitiors managed to develop a genuine relationship of mutual respect and friendship with great inequalities in their economic and military strength. In the aftermath of the 1962 confrontation, this imbalance may have been largely rectified, thus creating a new set of circumstances and presenting fresh opportunities for a renewal of the broken dialogue in the 1970's.

It appeared that such an opportunity was beginning to develop in 1970 when exploratory talks were held between Indian and Chinese diplomats in third country capitals, such as Cairo. Unfortunately, the developments in the then East Pakistan introduced new suspicions and tensions between India and China. Now that the crisis is left behind, the two neighbours and the relations between the three principals of the 1971 crisis, Bangladesh, Pakistan and India, have taken a cooperative attitude toward their mutual problems. It is my hope and expectation that new initiatives to normalize relations between India and China will go forward and bear fruit.

NOTES

1 Sisir Gupta, *India's Relations with Pakistan*, 1954-1957 (New Delhi : Indian Council of World Affairs, 1958), p. 1.
2 For a detailed discussion of Kashmir issue see Sisir Gupta, *Kashmir—A Study in India-Pakistan Relations* (New York and Bombay : Asia Publishing House, 1964); and K. Sarwar Hasan, *Pakistan and the United Nations* (New York : Manhattan Publishing Company, 1964). For an earlier but highly perceptive discussion of the involved issues see Joseph Korbel, *Danger in Kashmir* (Princeton, New Jersey : Princeton University Press, 1954).
3 Bhabani Sen Gupta, *The Fulcrum of Asia* (New York : Pegasus, 1970), p. 21.
4 *Jawaharlal Nehru's Speeches—1949-53* (Delhi : Publications Division, 1954), p. 296.
5 Even though India has followed a conscious policy of building a secular society, Pakistan has continued to view her neighbour in purely communal terms and had disregarded all empirical evidence to the contrary.
6 Khalid B. Sayeed, *The Political System of Pakistan* (Boston : Houghton-Mifflin Company, 1967), p. 263.
7 Walter Crocker, *Nehru: A Contemporary's Estimate* (London, 1966), pp. 92-93.
8 *Jawaharlal Nehru's Speeches—1946-1949* (Delhi : Publications Division, 1958), p. 73.
9 Jawaharlal Nehru, *The Unity of India* (New York, 1942), p. 223.
10 A. Campbell-Johnson, *Mission with Mountbatten* (London: Robert Hale, 1951), pp. 223-242.
11 *The Kashmir Question* (New Delhi : Ministry of External Affairs, 1956), p. 7.
12 For the full text of the resolution, *Ibid.* (Appendix II), pp. 31-33.
13 Josef Korbel, *Danger in Kashmir*, p. 25.
14 K. M. Panikkar, *India and China* (Bombay : Asia Publishing House, 1957), p. 15. Also see P. C. Chakravarti, *India's China Policy* (Bloomington, Indiana: Indiana University Press, 1962), p. 2.
15 Jawaharlal Nehru, *India's Foreign Policy* (Delhi: Publications Division, 1961), pp. 306-307.
16 *Khrushchev Remembers* (New York : Harper & Row, 1970).

[17] The India-China boundary question has been discussed in greater detail in many studies and documents. For an exhaustive treatment of the subject see *Notes, Memoranda and Letters Exchanged Between the Government of India and China* (White Papers *I* to *X*) (Delhi : Ministry of External Affairs, 1961 thru 1964). For an abridged version of the above, consult *The Sino-Indian Boundary* (New Delhi : Indian Society of International Law, 1962). For a legal Analysis of the dispute see R. S. Arora, "The Sino-Indian Border Dispute—A Legal Approach," *Public Law* (London : Summer, 1963), **pp.** 1-31. For a highly emotional and partisan Indian treatment of the military aspects of the border war, read Styanarayan Sinha, *China Strikes* (Delhi : Rama Krishna and Sons, 1964).

[18] For an interesting but greatly prejudiced British view of the India-China border war see Neville Maxwell, *India's China war* (London : Jonathan Cape Ltd., 1970).

CHAPTER VI

AN APPRAISAL

I BEGAN THIS study with a brief review of the various theories of international politics and foreign policy to emphasize the importance of and need for a theoretical foundation for an intelligent formulation and analysis of a nation's foreign relations. It must now be evident that I am committed to a "realist school" of international politics as the most appropriate theory to guide the foreign policy of a nation, in this instance, India. Three central concepts of this theory are worth repeating : (i) All politics are politics of interests—domestic or international; (ii) Power occupies a central place in the concept of interest; and (iii) Power relations are a dominant, though by no means exclusive, aspect of international politics.

The preceding review has led me to conclude that India's foreign policy has not followed a systematic or consistent path toward any well-defined national interests or objectives backed by adequate power. At best, it has been a continual groping for a middle ground for no convincing philosophical reasons; and, at worst, it may be characterized as utopian, naive, and disastrous for a nation of India's stature and potential power. In accordance with my *realpolitik* orientation, within the analytical framework outlined, let me now elaborate my general concerns and give some suggestions for change in India's foreign policy objectives.

A. NATIONAL OBJECTIVES AND COMMITMENTS

While international peace is essential for India's continued progress and development, India's capacity for promoting and maintaining such an international condition is nonetheless limited. I am reminded of a cartoon in *Shankar's Weekly* some years ago when Prime Minister Nehru paid visit to the United States. This cartoon showed President Eisenhower atop a skyscraper while Nehru had managed to soar to a similar height by means of the famous

Indian rope trick. The caption underneath teased: "Prime Minister Nehru and President Eisenhower had high-level talks." This cartoon contained an important message then and remains relevant today.

As indicated earlier, India's foreign policy has tended to operate in three concentric circles, namely: the superpowers, the Third World, and the neighbours. *The outermost circle received the most attention while the closest one received the least.* This state of affairs, more than any other, has been responsible for the nation's difficulties and is an indication of misplaced priorities.

At this juncture, three objectives must receive the highest priority from the nation's policy and decision-makers; these objectives include national security, national unity, and economic development. None of these objectives can be pursued separately, as they are inextricably linked with each other. India's national security is closely tied to the strength and viability of her national unity, and the prospects of her economic development depend heavily upon her national unity and security. The main purpose of India's foreign policy, therefore, above all else, must be the maintenance and promotion of these national priorities.

B. NATIONAL SECURITY AND FOREIGN POLICY

Until the Sino-Indian border conflict of October 1962, India followed a strict policy of non-alignment and, within its framework, did not accept any foreign military assistance. In a way, this approach, and the logic behind it, perpetrated the legal and moral fiction that such military aid precipitated regional arms races and intensified the Cold War. Meanwhile, India continued to use her own resources, which normally would have gone into economic projects, to maintain her military establishment and, in turn, used foreign assistance for economic development. It will be useful to remember that such a policy had been feasible only when India's security needs were interpreted by the Nehru government as limited. Nehru did not perceive any military threats to India from either the superpowers or immediate neighbours, except Pakistan. Consequently, he did not see the need for a large military capacity and readiness other than to meet any aggressive move from Pakistan. In short, the Indian military posture until 1962 was *status quo* posture and was directed toward maintaining a military superiority over Pakistan.

The Sino-Indian border conflict of 1962 marks a decisive departure from this *status quo* posture. In the years following the Chinese offensive, India's security needs have changed, both quantitatively and qualitatively. Today, India has over one million men under arms, compared with six hundred thousand in November 1962. Provided the current plans are fully implemented, this figure is scheduled to rise to some two million men. Table VI-1 shows how very costly this expansion is for India and the heavy burden it has placed upon her economy.

These figures illustrate three significant facts that deserve emphasis: (1) In per capita Gross National Product (GNP), India ranks 105th among the 120 countries included in the study; (2) But India's military establishment, with an expenditure of one and one-half billion dollars in 1967, placed her among the top ten nations of the world. This figure becomes still more significant when we realize that before 1962, India's entire defence budget amounted to a little over five hundred million dollars; and the 1971 defence expenditures reached two billion dollars; (3) The relative burden of India's military expenditure as a percentage of the nation's GNP for 1971 amounts to an excess of four per cent. This percentage is higher than that of many developed countries such as Canada (3.2%), Italy (3.2%), and Japan (.9%); and is comparable to that of some major powers such as France (5.1%), and West Germany (4.4%).

This rapid build-up of India's military establishment has created several problems. To begin with, it has committed a large amount of valuable human resources to the non-productive task of warfare. I am not concerned here about men who are ordinary soldiers, of whom India has plenty. What *is* important is that over 25,000 educated young men, many of whom are professionally trained technicians, have been drawn into the armed forces during the past four years alone. At the present juncture of India's development, these professional skills can certainly be put to better uses than the armed forces.

Secondly, the communications system from roads to rader leaves much to be desired and in the event of a confrontation with a major power such as China, it is not likely to prove equal to the task for the next several years.

Finally, and most importantly, the military equipment, despite

TABLE VI-1

RANKING OF MAJOR COUNTRIES ACCORDING TO GNP AND MILITARY EXPENDITURES

(Amounts in current dollars)

| | Gross national product | | | | Military-expenditures | | | |
| | Total | | Per capita | | Total | | Per capita | |
	Rank	Billion Dollars	Rank	Dollars	Rank	Billion Dollars	Rank	Dollars
United States*	1	793.5	1	3,985	1	75.5	1	379
Soviet Union*	2	384.0	19	1,630	2	52.0	2	221
West Germany	3	121.0	11	2,097	6	5.3	10	93
France*	4	115.9	8	2,323	4	5.9	5	117
Japan	5	115.7	25	1,158	13	1.1	58	11
United Kingdom*	6	110.9	15	2,014	5	6.4	7	117
Mainland China*	7	85.0	97	108	3	7.0	62	9
Italy	8	67.0	23	1,280	7	2.2	21	42
Canada	9	57.3	5	2,803	8	1.8	11	89
India	10	43.7	105	85	10	1.5	89	3
Poland	11	33.9	27	1,061	9	1.7	18	53
Brazil	12	29.7	53	347	15	.9	56	11
East Germany	13	28.8	18	1,780	18	.8	18	56
Spain	14	26.9	32	837	17	.8	34	25
Czechoslovakia	15	26.3	16	1,839	11	1.3	9	94
Australia	16	25.2	10	2,145	12	1.2	8	87

TABLE VI-1 (CONTINUED)

| | Gross national product | | | | Military-expenditures | | | |
| | Total | | Per capita | | Total | | Per capita | |
	Rank	Billion Dollars	Rank	Dollars	Rank	Billion Dollars	Rank	Dollars
Mexico.........	17	24.1	44	528	45	.2	78	4
Sweden.........	18	23.9	3	3,037	14	.9	4	120
Netherlands.....	19	22.7	17	1,802	16	.9	14	70
Belgium.........	20	19.5	14	2,035	22	.6	17	59
Romania........	21	18.8	29	975	20	.6	29	32
Switzerland.....	22	16.0	6	2,645	31	.4	16	62
Argentina......	23	14.9	37	649	39	.3	55	9
Pakistan........	24	13.7	96	113	25	.5	77	4
South Africa....	25	13.1	36	698	32	.4	38	20
Hungary........	26	12.6	24	1,234	42	.2	33	28
Denmark........	27	12.2	7	2,521	36	.3	15	62
Turkey.........	28	10.6	55	324	23	.5	48	16
Austria.........	29	10.6	22	1,447	47	.1	44	20
Yugoslavia......	30	9.7	46	487	30	.4	43	20

*Denotes country possessing nuclear weapons.

SOURCE: U. S. Arms Control and Disarmament Agency; *World Military Expenditures—1969.* (Washington, D. C., U. S. Government Printing Office), 1970, p. 20. Figures are for 1967, latest available as of this writing.

some marked improvements, is largely obsolete in the face of an adversary such as China and is likely to be outclassed in a major and prolonged conflict.

It is a truism that military strength must be a means to the achievement of political objectives and should never be allowed to become an end in itself. Therefore, if India's political objectives continue to remain a protracted confrontation with both of her neighbours, she will have to increase her resource commitment to these objectives accordingly. One approach to this problem now often heard in India, and which during the past few months has gained some backing in many powerful and influential circles, is that the defence and national security of the country lie in nuclear weapons. That this approach has some attraction to the Government of India is indicated by India's refusal to sign the nuclear non-proliferation treaty. Furthermore, several research institutes in India have produced rather detailed figures regarding the cost of producing nuclear weapons, the suggestion being that India could afford to acquire them without any undue hardship. Needless to say, India's decision to acquire nuclear weapons will not only be a reversal of her long-standing opposition to these devastating weapons but will also further exacerbate her relations with her neighbours, particularly China.[1]

There is, however, another solution to the problem of balancing resource commitments and foreign policy objectives. This is simply to bring the objectives in balance with available resources.

One of the cardinal principles of the "realist theory" of international politics is that commitments must follow interests and not vice versa. When I apply this principle to India's interests in terms of her two major neighbours, Pakistan and China, I fail to see the need for a continual confrontation with China. Moreover, it is virtually impossible to expect a rational policy from Pakistan toward India so long as Pakistan continues to remain obsessed with notions of being India's equal and a spokesman of the Muslims in the subcontinent. Sino-Indian relations, on the other hand, can definitely improve and can potentially be restored to their earlier friendly status. In my judgment, it is time that India broke away from the present non-productive confrontation stance toward China and made a dramatic move to settle the only real issue dividing the two neighbours, that is the boundary question. A beginning can be made by accepting Chou En-lai's 1960 offer to Nehru to swap the Chinese claims in Aksai Chin with India's claims in the N.E.F.A. along the McMahon Line. The benefits of such an accord can hardly be overstated. In addition to the potential of restoring India's relations with China, such a development will also put an end to Pakistan's mischief-making role in the region and will reduce India's dependence upon Soviet Union. All these objectives are not only desirable but essential if India is to be self-reliant and influential in the international community. In the year 1974, when even the United States, with its long history of hostility with China, is improving her relations with her, there is hardly any compelling reason for India not to do so.

C. NATIONAL UNITY AND FOREIGN POLICY

Despite the current slogan "unity in diversity," national unity and integration in India continue to be seriously handicapped as a result of conflicts arising out of religion, caste, language, and region. The danger to India's national existence that lies within these stresses and strains cannot be over-emphasized.

Even though India set out to build a secular, democratic republic from the moment of her independence in 1947, the goal of a a secular India still remains more of an ideal than an observable reality. Earlier in the study, I pointed out the importance of a truly secular national unity in India to combat the divisive Pakistani propaganda directed at many sensitive parts of India, especially the state of Jammu and Kashmir.

It is true that the Government of India is fairly impartial in her dealings with the religious groups in India and does not indulge in or encourage anti-religious activitives but in societal terms, the picture is not wholly satisfactory. Religious tolerance may be a more apt description of the current state of inter-religious relations in the country. This, obviously, is not enough. A significant change of direction within the entire society, particularly among the two major groups, the Hindus and the Muslims is urgently needed. In the absence of such a development, India's ability to pursue a successful foreign policy in many key areas of the world is likely to remain hampered.

I wish to emphasize that India's role and place in the world will be determined as much by what kind of society she builds at home as by what she does with her foreign policy. A dynamic,

vigorous, and secular society at home is bound to be conducive
to India's foreign policy objectives in the community of nations.
Needless to say, whatever the ideology or political orientation of
the Indian government, any neglect in the pursuit of a secular,
diverse, yet unified country from east to west and north to south
will only be an invitation to dissension and internal weakness.

D. ECONOMIC DEVELOPMENT AND FOREIGN POLICY

Time for India to achieve the economic transformation necessary
for her growth is constanly getting shorter. India must build an
independent, comprehensive, and modern industrial system and
put the economy, including agriculture, on a modern technical
basis within the next few years. Observers generally agree that
India's economic progress during the past two decades has been
slow if not unsatisfactory. During this period her overall industrial progress has been uneven. In some areas such as electricity,
oil refining, aviation, atomic energy, and some machine tools,
progress has been good ; but steel production and heavy industry
in general have not shown any major gains and, in view of the
growing demand, have actually fallen behind the performance
achieved in earlier years.

India's agricultural development is still far from sufficient. The
massive foreign assistance in food supplies to India (over 83.5
billion by the United States alone) bears testimony to the country's extreme dependence upon outside assistance (and possible
external pressure), although during the past few years India's
own supply of food has definitely increased. We should remember,
however, that the current "green revolution" is still confined to
only a few pockets in India and the general spreading of the
phenomenon may take many more years. Moreover, the delicate
state of the Indian economy demands that a vigorous and consistent drive for self-sufficiency be maintained under all circumstances. This observation further underlines my earlier comment
about accommodation with China in order to avoid the diversion
of any further resources into military commitments.

In many ways the success and failure of India as a major power
in Asia may well depend upon her ability to solve her own economic problems, particularly in agriculture and heavy industry. If
India can continue to move forward, a new image as an internally

stable, economically self-sufficient, and internationally significant nation will emerge. It will be both an appropriate and desirable image. India has a vital role to play in Asia, but it cannot be built upon platitudes. It must correspond to the nation's needs and interests and must be supported by appropriate resources and power. It is only after India establishes herself in Asia that the Third World and the super powers need to take India seriously and accord her appropriate status and position. Let me conclude this analysis by quoting an ancient Chinese proverb : *A Journey of a Thousand Miles Begins with the First Step*. In India, the first step calls for a re-evaluation of national priorities and objectives. It is time that Indian foreign policy operated within our three theoretical concentric circles in their logical order.

NOTES

1. For a detailed discussion on this point see N. C. Kasliwal, "Case Against Making an Atom Bomb," *People's Action* (New Delhi), September 1970.

POSTSCRIPT

INDIA'S EXPLOSION OF a nuclear device on 18 May 1974, has raised many significant questions for her foreign policy. I alluded to this likely development in my discussion of 'National Security and Foreign Policy' in the concluding chapter. Let me briefly discuss some implications of this nuclear explosion.

Despite the Government of India's repeated declarations that it's nuclear 'know-how' will be used for peaceful purposes only and that India has no intention of becoming a 'Nuclear Weapons Power,' the debate about "intentions" continues. Experts maintain that no distinction can be drawn between tests for peaceful purposes and those for arms development. In the words of the United States Arms Control and Disarmament Agency . . . "the technology of making nuclear explosive devices for peaceful purposes is indistinguishable from the technology of making nuclear weapons, and that nuclear weapons and nuclear explosive devices for peaceful purposes are both capable of releasing nuclear energy in an uncontrolled manner and have the common characteristics of large amounts of energy generated instantaneously from a compact source . . . ."[1]

This statement takes on added significance in the light of the fact that the Indian nuclear device was sophisticated enough and small enough to be lowered underground through a shaft. Consequently, a similar device, in all likelihood, can be easily carried aboard an airplane. Therefore, from a technical point it may be somewhat academic to attempt to differentiate between nuclear weapons and nuclear explosive devices, as well as, to sustain the distinction between a 'nuclear power' and a 'nuclear weapons power.' In other words, the real question is not whether India possesses nuclear devices or nuclear weapons but what she intends to do with them ?

Prime Minister Indira Gandhi's comment upon Indian nuclear explosion as "nothing to get excited about," will perhaps go down as an understatement of the year. I respect her political acumen and can appreciate the reasons for such a statement, as a development of such momentous proportions called for wisdom and restraint. The fact, however, remains that India's entry into the exclusive nuclear club, aside from a matter of some abstract national pride, contains the potential of radically altering the power-equation not only in Asia, but beyond. It remains to be seen whether, in the long run, the possession of nuclear devices will introduce new tensions and instability in India's relations with her immediate neighbours, China and Pakistan, or further the cause of political stability and peace.

Pakistan's initial reactions were both predictable and understandable. It was only a little over two years ago that Pakistan found itself reduced to the status of a small regional power. Her delusion to be India's rival and co-equal was shattered in the wake of the December 1971 India-Pakistan War and the emergence of Bangladesh. In view of such recent bitterness, Prime Minister Z.A. Bhutto may be forgiven for his melodramatic statements about Pakistani's "eating grass" to save resources to develop nuclear capability than to "accept Indian hegemony over the subcontinent."[2] Pakistani decision-makers must be fond of sheer fantasy to assume that India developed its nuclear capability to intimidate Pakistan. I remain hopeful that Mrs. Gandhi's assurances to Mr. Bhutto of India's continual desire to remain friendly and seek normalization of relations between the two countries would induce second thoughts in Islamabad, and the ongoing momentum toward reapproachment, though somewhat slower, would be maintained.

Perhaps the most significant development has been the Chinese "non-reaction" to India's nuclear explosion, and in it may lie the most hopeful sign to normalize Sino-Indian relations. Earlier in this book, I laid great stress to achieve this desirable objective and the reasons to do so have also been discussed. I have maintained that one of the most critical impediments to the normalization of Sino-Indian relations has been Chinese suspicion of India's 'quiet collusion' with the Soviet Union for a vairety of economic and military needs. Now that India has demonstrated her capability for self-sufficiency regarding her security needs, this should go a long way to allay Chinese suspicions and provide a basis for mutual trust leading to new initiatives to settle the outstanding boundary dispute.

The restoration of friendly relations on a basis of equality, mutual trust and benefit with China must remain the cornerstone of India's foreign policy. The nuclear genie must not be allowed to cloud this objective. A great deal of wisdom, restraint, and above all, patience, will be required.

The attainment of nuclear technology has opened many promising avenues for India. The development of closer relations between India and Iran particularly, holds great promise for the two countries, as well as, for the entire South and West Asia. The emerging special Indo-Iranian understandings and mutually beneficial joint economic ventures can go a long way in restoring not only the economic health of India, but can also for m a basis for a wider regional cooperation network of na tions including hopefully Pakistan and Afghanistan. I hope and trust that India's policy and decision-makers will conscientiously develop these options and utilize their nuclear technology to further the cause of stability and peace in the region.

NOTES

1. *U.S. Arms Control and Disarmament Agency-Publication 75* (Washington : D.C., U.S. Government Printing Office) 1974, P. 6.
2. *The Christian Science Monitor*, May 21, 1974. P. 3.

BIBLIOGRAPHY

THEORETICAL

BOASSON, CHARLES, *Approaches to the Study of International Relations*. Assen; The Netherlands : Van Gorcum, 1963.

BRECHER, MICHAEL, "International Relations and Asian Studies : The Subordinate State System of Southern Asia," *World Politics*, xv, January 1963, 213-235.

BULL, HEDLEY, "International Theory: The Case for a Classical Approach," *World Politics*, xviii, April 1966, 361-377.

COOK, THOMAS 1. AND MOOS, MALCOLM, *Power Through Purpose*. Baltimore : Johns Hopkins University Press, 1954.

FOX, WILLIAM, T. R., ed. *Theoretical Aspects of International Relations*. Notre Dame, Indiana : University of Notre Dame, 1959.

FRANKEL, JOSEPH, *The Making of Foreign Policy*. London: Oxford University Press, 1957.

GROSS, FELIKS, *Foreign Policy Analysis*. New York : Philosophical Library, 1954.

HAMILTON, WILLIAM C., "Some Problems of Decision-Making in Foreign Affairs," *Dept. of State Bulletin*, Vol. 37, Sept. 9, 1957.

HARRISON, HORACE, ed. *The Role of Theory in International Relations*. Princeton : D. Van Nostrand, 1964.

HOFFMAN, STANLEY, *Contemporary Theories in International Relations*. Englewood Cliffs, N. J. : Prentice-Hall, 1960.

——, *The State of War : Essays in the Theory and Practice of International Politics*. New York : Praeger, 1965.

——, "The Place of Theory in the Conduct and Study of International Relations," (Special issue) *Journal of Conflict Resolution*, iv, No. 3, 1960.

KAPLAN, MORTON A., *System and Process in International Politics*. New York : John Wiley & Sons, 1957.

KELMAN, HERBERT C., *International Behavior*, New York : Holt, Rinehart & Winston, 1965.

KLINEBERG, OTTO, *The Human Dimension in International Relations*. New York : Holt, Rinehart and Winston, 1964.

KNORR, K. AND VERBA, SIDNEY, eds. *The International System: Theoretical Essays*. Princeton : Princeton University Press, 1961.

LISKA, GEORGE, *International Equilibrium*, Cambridge: Harvard University Press, 1957.

LONDON, KURT, *The Making of Foreign Policy* : *East and West.* New York : J. B. Lippencott Co., 1965.

McCLELLAND, CHARLES A., "The function of Theory in International Relations." *Journal of Conflict Resolution,* IV, 1960, 303-336.
——, *Theory and the International System.* New York : Macmillan Company, 1966.

McCLOSKEY, HERBERT, "Perspectives on Personality and Foreign Policy." *World Politics,* XIII, 1961, 129-139.

MODELSKI, GEORGE A., *Theory of Foreign Policy.* New York : Frederick A. Praeger, 1961.

MORGENTHAU, HANS J., *Scientific Man Versus Power Politics.* Chicago : University of Chicago Press, 1946.
——, *In Defense of National Interest.* New York : Alfred Knopf, 1951.
——, *Politics Among Nations.* New York : Alfred Knopf, 3rd edition, 1960.
——, "Critical Look at the New Neutralism." *The New York Times Magazine,* August 27, 1961, 25.

PHIBBS, P. M., *Nehru's Philosophy of International Relations.* Chicago : University of Chicago, Unpublished Ph.D., Dissertation.

RANGE, WILLARD, *Jawaharlal Nehru's World View—A Theory of International Relations.* Athens : University of Georgia's Press, 1961.

ROSENAU, JAMES N., *Public Opinion and Foreign Policy—An Operational Formulation.* New York : Random House, 1961.
——, ed. *International Politics and Foreign Policy: A Reader in Research and Theory.* New York : Free Press of Glencoe, (1961), 1-75, 141-185, 412-448.
——, "Transforming the International System : Small Increments Along a Vast Periphery." *World Politics,* XVIII, April, 1966, 525-545.

RUSSETT, BRUCE M., *Trends in World Politics.* New York : Macmillan Company 1965.

SCHELLING, THOMAS C., *The Strategy of Conflict.* New York : Oxford University Press (Galaxy Paperback), 1963.

SHEY, THEODORE L., "Non-alignment Yes, Neutralism No." *Review of Politics,* Vol. 30, No. 2, April, 1968, 228-245.

SINGER, J. DAVID, "The Relevance of the Behavioral Sciences to the Study of International Relations." *Behavioral Science,* Vol. 3, 1958, 278-284.
——, *Human Behavior and International Politics.* Chicago : Rand McNally, 1965.

SINGH, BALJIT, "The Sources of Contemporary Political Thought in India— A Reappraisal." *Ethics,* Vol. LXXV, No. 1, October, 1964, 57-62.
——, "The Quest for Theory in International Relations." *The Indian Journal of Political Science,* Vol. XXVII, No. 2, April-June, 1966, 1-11.

SNYDER, RICHARD C. AND ROBINSON, JAMES A., *National and International Decision-Making.* New York : The Institute for International Order, 1961.
——, BRUCK, N. W. AND SAPIN, BURT, *Foreign Policy Decision-Making : An Approach to the Study of International Politics.* New York : Free Press, 1962.

Symposium on Neutrality—*United Asia,* Vol. 13, No. 3. 145-79.

THOMPSON, KENNETH W., *Political Realism and the Crisis of World Politics*. Princeton : Princeton University Press, 1960.

GENERAL AND HISTORICAL

APPADORAI, A., "On Understanding Indian Foreign Policy." *International Relations*. October, 1960.

AZAD, MAULANA ABUL KALAM, *India Wins Freedom*, an autobiographical narrative, Bombay : 1959.

BAINS, J.S., *India's International Disputes : A Legal Study*. Bombay, New York : Asia Publishing House, 1962.

BERKES, ROSS N. AND BEDI, MOHINDER S., *Diplomacy of India*. Stanford : Stanford University Press, 1958.

BERKES, ROSS N., "India and the Communist World." *Current History*, Vol. 36, No. 211, March, 1959.

"The Bomb." *Seminar* Vol. 65 (January, 1965), 11-56. Symposium participants : A. D. Moddie, H. M. Patel, Raj Krishna, Analyst, pseud., Sisir Gupta, Seminarist, pseud., Romesh Thapar and R. K. Nehru. Contains a bibliography.

BOZEMAN, ADDA, "India's Foreign Policy Today : Reflections Upon Its Sources." *World Politics*, Vol. x, January, 1958, 256-273.

BRECHER, MICHAEL, *Nehru : A Political Biography*. New York : Oxford University Press, 1959.

——, "Neutralism : An Analysis." *International Journal* Vol. xvii, Summer, 1962, 224-36.

——, *India and the World Politics—Krishna Menon's View of the World*. London : Oxford University Press, 1968.

BRODIE, H., *South Asia in the World Today*. Chicago : University of Chicago Press, 1950.

CAMPBELL-JOHNSON, A., *Mission with Mountbatten*. London : Robert Hale, 1951.

CHAGLA, M.C., *An Ambassador Speaks*. New York: Asia Publishing House, 1962.

CHAWLA, S., *India, Russia and China, 1947-1955*. Ann Arbor : University Microfilms, Microfilm AC-1, No. 59-2734. An interpretation of the Indian Concept of national interest.

CAIPMAN, WARWICK, *India's Foreign Policy*. Toronto : Candian Institute of International Affairs, 1954.

CROCKER, WALTER, *Nehru : A Contemporary's Estimate*. London: 1966.

DEAN, VERA MICHELES, "World and India at Three-pronged Cross-roads." *Indian and Foreign Review*, Vol. 4, No. 10, March 1, 1967, 10, 18.

DEVDUTT, "Non-alignment and India." *The Indian Journal of Political Science*, Vol. 23, No. 4, October-December, 1962.

EDWARDS, MICHAEL, "Illusion and Reality in India's Foreign Policy." *International Affairs*, Vol. 41, No. 1, January, 1965, 48-58.

——, "India, Pakistan and Nuclear Weapons." *International Affairs*, Vol. 43, No. 4u, October, 1967, 655-663.

FONTERA, RICHARD M., "Anti-Colonialism as a Basic Indian Foreign Policy." *Western Political Quarterly*, Vol. 13, June, 1960, 421-432.

GOPAL, MADAN, *India as World Power*. Delhi : Rajkamal Publications, 1948.
Government of India, Ministry of External Affairs. *Toward Peace and Better Understanding*. Delhi : Publications Division, 1955.
GUPTA, BHABANI SEN, *The Fulcrum of Asia*. New York : Pegasus, 1970.

KAMATH, M. V., "India's Dynamic Neutralism." *Current History*, XXXVI, March, 1959, 135-140.
KARUNAKARAN, K. P., *India in World Affairs*. 2 Vols. New York : Oxford University Press, 1958.
——, *Alignment and Non-alignment in Asia*. New Delhi : Peoples Publishing House, 1961.
——, ed., *Outside the Contest*. New Delhi : Peoples Publishing House, 1963.
Khrushchev Remembers. New York : Harper & Row, 1970.
KRIPALANI, J. B., "For Principled Neutrality." *Foreign Affairs*. XXVIII, October, 1959, 46-60.
KUNDRA, JAGDISH, *Indian Foreign Policy : 1947-1954—A Study of Relations with the Western Bloc*. New York : Gregory Lounz, 1953.

LEVI, WERNER, *Free India in Asia*. Minneapolis : University of Minnesota Press, 1952.
LOHIA, R., *The Third Camp in World Affairs*. Bombay : Madhu Limaye for the Socialist Party, 1951.
Lok Sabha Secretariat, *Foreign Policy of India : Texts of Documents*. New Delhi : 1958.
LYON, PETER, "India's Foreign Policy—Interplay of Domestic and External Factors." *South Asian Studies*, Vol. 4, No. 1, January, 1969, 1-25.

MALENBAUM, WILFRED, *East and West in India's Development*. National Planning Association, 1959.
MALLIK, DEVA NARAYAN, *The Development of Non-alignment in India's Foreign Policy*. Allahabad : Chaitanya Publishing House, 1967.
MEHTA, ASHO: 'India's Foreign Policy." *India Quarterly*, Vol. VII, No. 1, April-June, 1951, 99-165.
MEHTA, G. L., *Understanding India*. New York : Asia Publishing House, 1961.
MENDE, TIBOR, *Nehru : Conversations on India and World Affairs*. New York : George Braziller, Inc., 1956.
MIKSCHE, F. O., "The Arms Race in the Third World." *Orbis*, Vol. 12, No. 1, Spring, 1968, 161-166.
MILIC, N., "India in Today's World." *Review of International Affairs* Vol. 1, 8, No. 422, November 5, 1967, 8-11.
MURTI, B. S. N., *Nehru's Foreign Policy*. New Delhi : Beacon Information and Publications, 1953.

NAIR, KUSUM, "Where India, China and Russia Meet." *Foreign Affairs*, Vol. 36, No. 2. January, 1958.

NEHRU, JAWAHARLAL, *India's Foreign Policy—Selected Speeches*, September 1946-April 1961, Delhi : Publications Division, Government of India, 1961.

NEHRU, JAWAHARLAL, TOYNBEE, ARNOLD AND ATTLEE, EARL, *India and the World*. New Delhi : Allied Publishers, 1962.

NEHRU, JAWAHARLAL, "Changing India." *Foreign Affairs*, Vol. 41, No. 3, April, 1963.

NIXON, RICHARD M., *U. S. Foreign Policy for the 1970's ; A New Strategy for Peace*. Washington, D. C., 1970.

PALMER, NORMAN D., "India's Outlook on Foreign Affairs." *Current History*, xxx, No. 174, February, 1956, 65-72.

——, "India Faces a New Decade." *Current History*, March, 1961, Vol. 40, 147-152.

——, "India's Foreign Policy." *The Political Quarterly*. October-December, 1962.

PANIKKAR, K. M., *A Survey of India History*. Bombay : Asia Publishing House, 1956.

PARAMESHWARAN, C., "The Growing Ascendency of Pro-Communist, Pro-Soviet Forces in India." *Revue Militaire Generale*, February, 1964.

PATEL, S. R., *Foreign Policy of India : An Inquiry and Criticism*. Bombay : N. M. Tripathi, 1960.

PHILIPS, C. H., ed. *Politics and Society in India*: New York : Praeger, 1962.

POPLAI, S. L., ed. *The Temper of Peace*. New Delhi : Indian Council of World Affairs, 1955.

——, ed. *India : 1947-1950* (2 Volumes Internal Affairs and External Affairs). London : Oxford University Press, 1959.

POWER, PAUL F., ed. *India's Non-alingment Policy—Strengths and Weaknesess*. Boston : D. C. Health, 1967.

PRASAD, BIMLA, "A Fresh Look at India's Foreign Policy." *International Studies*, Vol. 8, No. 3, January, 1967, 277-299.

QURESHI, KHALIDA, "Arms Aid to India and Pakistan." *Pakistan Horizon*, Vol. 20, No. 2, 1967, 137-150.

RAJAGOPALACHARI, C., "The Contradictions in Nehru's World Policy." *Swarajya*, Vol. 5, No. 39, April, 1961.

RAJKUMAR, N. V., *The Background of India's Foreign Policy*. New Delhi: All India Congress Committee, 1962.

SALETORE, B. A., *India's Diplomatic Relations with the East*. Bombay : Popular Book Depot, 1960.

SCALAPINO, ROBERT, "Moscow, Peking and the Communist Parties of Asia." *Foreign Affairs*. January, 1963.

SEN, CHANAKYA, *Against the Cold War*. New York : Asia Publishing House, 1962.

SHULMAN, MARSHALL D., *Stalin's Foreign Policy Reappraised*. Cambridge, Mass.: Harvard University Press, 1963.

SINGH, BALJIT, "The End of the Nehru Era." *Eastern World*. London, Vol.

xviii, October, 1964, No. 10, 11-15.

——, "Pundits and Punchsheela : Indian Intellectuals and Their Foreign Policy." *International Studies Quarterly*. Formerly Background Vol. ix, No. 3, August, 1965, 127-136.

——, "India's Triple Dilemma." *United Asia* (Special 20th Anniversary issue, January, 1968), 12-16.

Singh, Patwant, *India and the Future of Asia*. London : Faber and Faber, 1966.

Smith, Donald Eugene, *India as a Secular State*. Princeton, New Jersey : Princeton University Press, 1963.

Sondhi, M. L., "Seminar on Nuclear Weapons and Foreign Policy." *International Studies*, Vol. 9, No. 2, October 1967, 151-161.

Thayer, Philip W., ed. *Nationalism and Progress in Free Asia*. Baltimore : The John Hopkins Press, 1956.

Tinker, Hugh, "Magnificient Failure ? The Gandhian Ideal in India After Sixteen Years." *International Affairs*, April, 1964.

Verghese, B. G., "A Reassessment of Indian Policy in Asia." *India Quarterly*. April, 1961, 17.

Wallbank, Walter T., *A Short History of India and Pakistan*. New York : The New American Library—A Mentor Book, 1958.

Ward, Barbara, *The Interplay of East and West* . New York : W. W. Norton and Company, 1962.

Zinkin, Maurice and Ward, Barbara, *Why Help India ?* New York : The Macmillan Co., 1963.

Zinkin, Taya, "Indian Foreign Policy : An Interpretation of Attitudes." *World Politics*, January, 1955, vii, No. 2, 179-208.

INDIA AND THE SUPER POWERS

Akhminov, H., "Indians and the Soviet Union." *Bulletin of the Institute for the Study of the USSR*. April, 1961.

Arora, S. K., *American Foreign Policy Towards India*. New Delhi : Suneja Book Centre, 1954.

Balabushevich, V. V. and Prasad, Bimla, eds. *India and the Soviet Union*. Delhi : Peoples Publishing House, 1969.

Bowles, Chester, *Ambassador's Report*. New York : Harper, 1954.

Brown, Norman W., *The United States and India and Pakistan*. Cambridge, Mass. : Harvard University Press, 1963.

N. A. Bulganin and N. S. Khrushchev in India. San Francisco : American-Russian Institute, 1956.

Chakravarti, P. C., "Indian Non-alignment and the United States Policy." *Current History*, Vol. 41, March, 1963, 129-134.

CRABB, CECIL, "American Diplomatic Tactics and Neutralism." *Political Science Quarterly,* LXXVIII, No. 3, 1963.

DESAI, ASHOK V., "India's Growing Military Problems—Reaching Out to the Soviet Union." *Round Table,* Vol. 228, October, 1967, 369-379.

GUPTA, SISIR, "India and the Soviet Union." *Current History,* Vol. 44, March, 1963, 141-146.

HARRISON, SELIG S., ed. *India and the United States.* New York : Macmillan, 1961.

"Indo-Soviet Link." *Seminar,* Vol. 73, September, 1965, 10-46. Symposium Participants : Harish Kapur, P. L. Joshi, Balraj Madhok, K. P. S. Menon, Sisir Gupta and D. K. Rangnekar. Contains a bibliography.

KULKARNI, MAYA, *Indo-Soviet Political Relations Since the Bandung Conference of 1955.* Bombay : Vora and Co., 1968.
KUMAR, VIJAY, *Anglo-American Plot Against Kashmir.* New Delhi : Peoples Publishing House, 1962.

MARKEL, LESTER, "The Myths that Divide India and U.S." *New York Times Magazine,* Vol. 29, January 15, 1967, 92-96.

NAIK, J. A., *Soviet Policy Toward India—From Stalin to Brezhnev.* Delhi : Vikas Publications, 1970.
NATARAJAN, L., *American Shadow over India* with a forward by J. C. Kumarappa. Bombay : Peoples Publishing House, 1952.
NEHRU, J., *Visit to America.* New York : John Day Co., 1950.

PALMER, NORMAN D, "India and the United States : Maturing Relations." *Current History,* Vol. 36, March, 1959, 129-134.
——, *South Asia and the United States Policy.* Boston, Mass., Houghton Mifflin Company, 1966.

Rana, Rahu Nath, "The Soviet Attitude Towards Colonialism with special Reference to India." *Indian Journal of Political Science,* Vol. 29, No. 2, April-June, 1968, 114-126.
ROSINGER, L. K., *India and the United States.* New York : Macmillan, 1950.

SAKSENA, VIMLA, *India's Relations with Soviet Union, 1959-65.* The Hague : Martinus Nijhoff, 1966.
SINGH, BALJIT, "The United States and the India-Pakistan Conflict." *Parliamentary Studies,* Vol. IX, No. 12, December, 1965, 15-19.
SPEAR, T. G. P., *India, Pakistan and the West.* New York : Oxford University Press, 1958.
STEIN, ARTHUR, "India and the USSR—Post-Nehru Period." *Asian Survey,* Vol. 7, No. 3, March, 1967, 165-175.

——, *India and the Soviet Union*. Chicago : University of Chicago Press, 1969.

Talbot, Phillips and Poplai, S. L., *India and America : A Study of Their Relations*. New York : Harper and Brother, 1958.

Tarr, David W., *American Strategy in the Nuclear Age*. New York : Macmillan, 1966.

Ward, Barbara, *India and the West*. New York : Norton & Co., 1961.

INDIA AND THE THIRD WORLD

Appadorai, A., "The Bandung Conference." *India Quarterly*, xl, No. 3, July-September, 1955, 207-235. Also printed as a pamphlet by the Indian Council of World Affairs, New Delhi.

Dadoo, Y. M., "Role of the Indians in the South African Revolution." *People's Democracy*, Vol. 4, No. 27, July 7, 1968, 4, 10.

Emerging World, The, *Jawaharlal Nehru Memorial Volume*. New York : Asia Publishing House, 1964.

Extracts of Statements Explaining India's Views on Vietnam. Washington, D. C.: Information Services of India.

Ghosh, Ajoy, "The Bandung Conference." *Political Affairs*, xxxiv, No. 6, June, 1955, 13-19.

Gupta, Anirudha, "Assessing the Reality in Africa—an Indian Point of View." *Economic and Political Weekly*, Vol. 3, No. 19, May, 11, 1968, 751-755.

Hendre, S., *India and the Bandung Conference*. Bombay : Planning for Democracy Series, No. 1, 1955.

"Indians in Africa." *Seminar*, Vol. 10, January, 1960, 12-47. Symposium participants : D. K. Sharda, A. Oginga Odinga, R. B. Pandya, Basil Davidson, Mukul Mukherjee and D. C. Carver. Contains a select bibliography.

Khan, Rahmatullah, "India and the Decolonization of Africa." *Africa Quarterly*, Vol. 8, No. 3, October-December, 1968, 238-246.

Korey, William, "India and Israel—Unmasking a Neutral." *New Leader*, Vol. 50, No. 15, July 17, 1967, 6-9.

Kozicki, Richard J., "Indian Policy Toward the Middle East." *Orbis*, Vol. 11, No. 3, Fall, 1967, 786-797.

Marvin, David K., *Emerging Africa in World Affairs*. San Francisco, California : Chandler Publishing Company, 1965.

Menon, V. K. Krishna, "The Israeli Aggression Against the Arab Countries." *Afro-Asian and World Affairs*. Vol. 4, No. 3, Autumn, 1967, 185-203.

Misra, K. P., "Recognition of the Algerian Republic : A Study of the

Policy and Government of India." *Political Studies*, June, 1962.

"Neutral Summit." *Eastern Economist*, Vol. 37, No. 10, September 8, 1961, 436-437.

PANIKKAR, K.M., *The Afro-Asian States and Their Problems*. New York : Day, 1959.
POWER, PAUL F., "India and Vietnam." *Asian Survey*, Vol. 7, No. 10, October, 1967, 740-751.

SARDESAI, D. R., *Indian Foreign Policy in Cambodia, Laos, and Vietnam, 1947-64*. Berkeley : University of California, 1968.
SHARABI, HISHAM B., *Nationalism and Revolution in the Arab World*. Princeton, N. J. : D. Van Nostrand, 1966.
SINGH, BALJIT, "India's Policy and the Vietnam Conflict." *World Affairs*, Vol. 129, No. 4, January-March, 1967, 251-255.

TON, THAT THIEN, *India and South East Asia 1947-1960*. Genieve : Librairie Broz, 1963.

INDIA AND HER NEIGHBOURS

AL-MUJAHID, SHARIF, "India's Attitude Towards Pakistan." *Pakistan Horizon*, No. 9, 1961, 320-322.
ANWAR, SYED, "The Politics of Sino-Pakistan Agreements." *Orbis*, Vol. 11, No. 3, Fall, 1967, 798-825.
ARMSTRONG, HAMILTON FISH, "Where India Faces China." *Foreign Affairs*, Vol. 37, July, 1959, 617-625.
"Asian Security." *Seminar* Vol. 8, No. 96, August, 1967, 10-47. Participants : Sisir Gupta, Shiv K. Shastri, Romesh Thapar, S. Gopal, Girilal Jain and M. S. Venkataramani. Contains a select bibliography.

BARAETT, A. DOAK, *Communist China and Asia*. New York : Vintage Books, 1961.
"Between Delhi and Peking." *Round Table*, December, 1962.
BHARGAVA, G. S., "A Balanced China Policy." *Economic and Political Weekly*, Vol. 2, No. 39, September 30, 1967, 1756-1757.
BHAT, SUDHAKAR, *India and China*. New Delhi : Popular Book Service, 1967.
BINDER, LEONARD, *Religion and Politics in Pakistan*. Berkeley, California : University of California Press, 1961.
BIRDWOOD, C. B. B., *India and Pakistan : A Continent Decides*. New York : Praeger, 1974.
———, *Two Nations and Kashmir*. London : R. Hale, 1956.
BOYD, R. G., *Communist China's Foreign Policy*. New York : Praeger, 1962.
BRINES, RUSSEL, *The Indo-Pakistani Conflict*. London : Pall Mall Press, 1968.
BRIGHT, J. S., *Ceylon Kicks India*. New Delhi : Chaudhry Knowledge Empor um, 1950.

CALLARD, KIETH, *Political Forces in Pakistan*. New York : Inst. of Pacific Relations, 1959.

CAROE, SIR OLAF, "The Indian-Chinese Boundary Dispute." *Geographical Journal*, September, 1961, 345-346.

CHAKRAVARTI, P. C., *India's China Policy*. Bloomington : Indiana University Press, 1962.

CHANDRASEKHAR, S., "Sino-Indian Relations." *Antioch Review*, Vol. 20, Fall, 1960, 296-307.

"China." *Seminar* Vol. 50, October, 1963, 10-67. Symposium participants, Karunakar Gupta, Mohit Sen, Vidya Prakash Dutt, Basanti Mitra, M. K. Thavaraj, Rasheeduddin Khan and John Robinson. Contains a bibliography.

"Chinese Aggression and India." *International Studies*, Vol. v, No. 1 and 2, July-October, 1963, Special Issue.

DALVI, J. P., *Himalayan Blunder*. Bombay : Thacker, 1969.

DAS-GUPTA, J. B., *Indo-Pakistan Relations, 1947-1955*. New York : Gregory Lounz, 1958.

DESAI, W. S., *India and Burma : A Study*. Bombay : Orient Longmans under the auspices of the Indian Council of World Affairs, 1954.

Documents on the Sino-Indian Boundry Question. Peking : Foreign Language Press, 1960.

DUPREE, LOUIS, "India's State in Afghan-Pakistan Relations." *American Universities Field Staff Report Studies*. South Asia Series, Vol. vi, No. 1.

FISHER, M. AND BONDURANT, J. V., *Indian View of the Sino-Indian Relations*. Berkeley : Institute of International Relations, University of California, 1956.

FISHER, MARGARET AND ROSE, LEO, "Ladakh and the Sino-Indian Border Crisis." *Asian Survey*, Vol. 2, No. 8, October, 1962, 27.

"Geopolotics of the Himalayan Region." *United Asia*, Vol. 12, No. 4, 1960, 306-394.

GRAEBNER, A. Norman, "China and Asian Security—An American Dilemma." *International Journal*, Vol. 16, 1961, 213-230.

GUPTA, BHABANI SEN, "A Maoist Line for India." *China Quarterly*, Vol. 33, January-March, 1968, 3-16.

GUPTA SISIR, "The Nehru-Ayub Meeting." *Foreign Affairs Reports*. October, 1960, 122-133.

——, *Kashmir—A Study in India-Pakistan Relations*. New York and Bombay : Asia Publishing House, 1964.

HANSEN, G. ERIC, "Indian Perceptions of the Chinese Communist Regime and Revolution." *Orbis*, Vol. 12, No. 1, Spring, 1968, 268-293.

HASAN, K. SARWAR, *Pakistan and the United Nations*. New York : Manhattan Publishing Co., 1964.

HUSSAIN, KARKI, "China's Image of India's Foreign Policy of Non-alignment." *The Indian Journal of Political Science*, Vol. 23, No. 3, July-September, 1962.

"India, China and Japan : The Emerging Balance in Asia." *Orbis*, Vol. 1, No. 14, Winter, 1958.

"India and Her Neighbors : Hostility on Right and Left." *Round Table*, September, 1956, 184.

'India and Pakistan," *Seminar*, Vol. 48, August, 1963, 10-51. Symposium participants : Prem Chopra, Satish Chandra, Khalid Sayeed, Sisir Gupta, Ashok Mitra, Balraj Puri, and Maj-Gen. Habibullah. Contains a bibliography.

THE INDIAN SOCIETY of International Law, *The Sino-Indian Boundry—Text of Treaties, Agreements and Certain Exchange of Notes Relating to the Sino-Indian Boundary*. Delhi : Central Electric Press, 1962.

JAIN, GIRILAL, *India Meets China in Nepal*. Bombay : Asia Publishing House, 1959.

——, *Panchsheela and After : A Reappraisal of Sino-Indian Relations in the Contexts of the Tibetan Insurrection*. New York : Asia Publishing House, 1961.

JOHRI, SITA RAM, *Chinese Invasion of NEFA*. Lucknow : Himalaya Publications, 1968.

KARAN, P. P., "Bhutan and Sikkim : Himalayan Shangri-La, Now Darkened by Communist China's Shadow, Faces Upto the 20th Century." *Canadian Geographical Journal*, Vol. 65, December, 1962, 200-209.

KHAN, MOHAMMAD AYUB, *Pakistan Perspective*, Washington, D. C. : Embassy of Pakistan, 1965.

——, *Friends Not Masters*. London : Oxford University Press, 1967.

KORBEL, JOSEF, *Danger in Kashmir*. Princeton, New Jersey : Princeton University Press, 1966. Revised Edition.

KUO-CHUN, CHAO, "The Chinese-Indian Controversy." *Current History*, Vol. 37, No. 220, December, 1959, 354-361.

LAKHANPAL, P. L., *Essential Documents and Notes on Kashmir Dispute*. New Delhi : International Publications, 1958.

LAL, MUKAT BEHARI, *Communist China's Aggression*. New Delhi : Peoples Publishing House, 1959.

LEVI, W., "Pakistan, the Soviet Union and China." *Pacific Affairs*, Fall, 1962.

MISRA, K. P., "Indo-Afghan Relations." *South Asian Studies*, Vol. 2, No. 1, January, 1967, 59-70

MAXWELL, NEVILLE, *India's China War*. London : Jonathan Cape Ltd., 1970.

MENON, V. K. KRISHNA, *Text of Address at the United Nations Tenth Anniversary Meeting, June, 1955*. San Francisco : Distributed by the Consulate-General of India, mimeographed.

——, *Kashmir*. New Delhi : Publications Division, January-February, 1957.

——, *India and the Chinese Invasion*. Bombay : Contemporary Publishers, 1963.

Ministry of External Affairs, Government of India, *Prime Minister on Sino-Indian Relations. Vol. 1 : In Parliament*. New Delhi : Government of India Press, 1961.

——, *Prime Minister on Sino-Indian Relations, Vol. 11, Press Conferences*. New Delhi:

Government of India Press, 1961.

——, *Notes, Memoranda and Letters Exchanged Between the Governments of India and China*. White Papers, New Delhi : Government of India Press, Vol. 1, 1954-59, 1959; Vol. 11, September-November, 1959, 1959; Vol. 111, November, 1959-March, 1960, 1960; Vol. iv, March, 1960-November, 1960, 1960; Vol. v, November, 1960-November, 1961, 1961; Vol. vi, November, 1961-July, 1962, 1962; Vol. vii, July, 1962-October, 1962, 1962.

——, *India-China Border Problem*. New Delhi : Government of India Press, 1962.

——, *Leading Events in India-China Relations, 1947-1962*. New Delhi : Government of India Press, 1962.

——, *World Press on Chinese Aggression*. New Delhi : Government of India Press, 1962.

——, *Nehru's Letter to Chou En-lai, November 14, 1962*. New Delhi : Government of India Press, 1962.

——, *Nehru Writes to Heads of States*. New Delhi : Government of India Press, 1962.

——, *Indian Communists Condemn Chinese Aggression*. New Delhi : Government of India Press, 1962.

PANIKKAR, K. M., *India and China*. Bombay : Asia Publishing House, 1957.

PALMER, NORMAN D., "Pakistan's Mood : The New Realism." *Current History*. November, 1962.

——, "Trans-Himalayan Confrontation." *Orbis*, Vol. 6, Winter, 1963, 513-527.

PRASAD, BIMLA, "A Fresh Approach to India-Pakistan Relations." *South Asian Studies*, Vol. 2, No. 2, July, 1967, 167-170.

Publications Division, *A Nation Aroused—How India is Determined to Fight China's Aggression*. Faridabad : Government of India Press, 1962.

——, *Menace to India's Freedom—How China Has Violated Agreements and Has Now Invaded Our Sacred Land*. Faridabad : Government of India Press, November, 1962.

ROSE, LEO E., "Nepal : The Quiet Monarch." *Asian Survey*, February, 1964.

Seminar on India's Relations with China, 1967. Working papers. New Delhi : Indian School of International Studies, 1967.

SETH, S. P., "China as a Factor in Indo-Pakistani Politics." *World Today*, Vol. 25, No. 1, January, 1967, 36-46.

SHELVANKAR, K. S. AND AHMED, N., "China's Himalayan Frontiers." *International Affairs*, October, 1962.

SHERWANI, LATIF AHMAD, *India, China and Pakistan*. Karachi : Council for Pakistan Studies, 1967.

SIMON, SHELDON W., "The Kashmir Dispute in Sino-Soviet Perspective." *Asian Survey*, Vol. 7, No. 3, March, 1957, 176-187.

SINHA, SATYANARAYAN, *China Strikes*. Delhi : Rama Krishna and Sons, 1964.

SINGH, BALJIT, "National Unity and the Pattern of Democracy in India." *Parliamentary Studies*. Vol. 9, Nos. 6-7, June-July, 1965, 19-23. Reprinted in *Eastern World*, Vol. xix, No. 12, December, 1965, 13-14.

SINGH, BISHWANATH, "The Legality of McMahon Line—Indian Perspective."
 Orbis, Vol. 11, No. 1, Spring, 1967, 271-284.

——, "Kutch Award—A Study in Indo-Pakistan Relations." *Indian Journal
of Political Science*, Vol. 29, No. 2, April/June, 1968, 155-162.

SINGH, HARMANDAR, ed. *India and Her Neighbours*. Jullundur : Books International,
 1967.

SINGH, SANGAT, *Pakistan's Foreign Policy*. New York : Asia Publishing House,
 1970.

The Sino-Indian Boundary. New Delhi : Indian Society of International Law,
 1962,

SURJEET, HARKISHEN SINGH, *Kashmir and Its Future*. New Delhi : Peoples Publishing House, 1962.

The Tashkent Declaration. New Delhi : Publications Div., Government of India,
 1966.

WILCOX, WAYNE AYRES, *India, Pakistan and the Rise of China*. New York :
 Walker, 1964.

INDEX